SECOND EDITION

Measuring the

Performance of Human Service Programs

SAGE HUMAN SERVICES GUIDES

A series of books edited by ARMAND LAUFFER and CHARLES D. GARVIN. Published in cooperation with the University of Michigan School of Social Work and other organizations.

1: **GRANTSMANSHIP** by Armand Lauffer (second edition)

2: **CREATING GROUPS** by Harvey J. Bertcher and Frank F. Maple (second edition)

10: **GROUP PARTICIPATION** by Harvey J. Bertcher (second edition)

11: **BE ASSERTIVE** by Sandra Stone Sundel and Martin Sundel

14: **NEEDS ASSESSMENT** by Keith A. Neuber with William T. Atkins, James A. Jacobson, and Nicholas A. Reuterman

15: **DEVELOPING CASEWORK SKILLS** by James A. Pippin

17: **EFFECTIVE MEETINGS** by John E. Tropman (second edition)

20: **CHANGING ORGANIZATIONS AND COMMUNITY PROGRAMS** by Jack Rothman, John L. Erlich, and Joseph G. Teresa

25: **HELPING WOMEN COPE WITH GRIEF** by Phyllis P. Silverman

29: **EVALUATING YOUR AGENCY'S PROGRAMS** by Michael J. Austin, Gary Cox, Naomi Gottlieb, J. David Hawkins, Jean M. Kruzich, and Ronald Rauch

30: **ASSESSMENT TOOLS** by Armand Lauffer

31: **UNDERSTANDING PROGRAM EVALUATION** by Leonard Rutman and George Mowbray

33: **FAMILY ASSESSMENT** by Adele M. Holman

35: **SUPERVISION** by Eileen Gambrill and Theodore J. Stein

37: **STRESS MANAGEMENT FOR HUMAN SERVICES** by Richard E. Farmer, Lynn Hunt Monohan, and Reinhold W. Hekeler

38: **FAMILY CAREGIVERS AND DEPENDENT ELDERLY** by Dianne Springer and Timothy H. Brubaker

39: **DESIGNING AND IMPLEMENTING PROCEDURES FOR HEALTH AND HUMAN SERVICES** by Morris Schaefer

40: **GROUP THERAPY WITH ALCOHOLICS** by Baruch Levine and Virginia Gallogly

41: **DYNAMIC INTERVIEWING** by Frank F. Maple

43: **CAREERS, COLLEAGUES, AND CONFLICTS** by Armand Lauffer

45: **TREATING ANXIETY DISORDERS** by Bruce A. Thyer

46: **TREATING ALCOHOLISM** by Norman K. Denzin

47: **WORKING UNDER THE SAFETY NET** by Steve Burghardt and Michael Fabricant

48: **MANAGING HUMAN SERVICES PERSONNEL** by Peter J. Pecora and Michael J. Austin

49: **IMPLEMENTING CHANGE IN SERVICE PROGRAMS** by Morris Schaefer

50: **PLANNING FOR RESEARCH** by Raymond M. Berger and Michael A. Patchner

51: **IMPLEMENTING THE RESEARCH PLAN** by Raymond M. Berger and Michael A. Patchner

52: **MANAGING CONFLICT** by Herb Bisno

53: **STRATEGIES FOR HELPING VICTIMS OF ELDER MISTREATMENT** by Risa S. Breckman and Ronald D. Adelman

54: **COMPUTERIZING YOUR AGENCY'S INFORMATION SYSTEM** by Denise E. Bronson, Donald C. Pelz, and Eileen Trzcinski

55: **HOW PERSONAL GROWTH AND TASK GROUPS WORK** by Robert K. Conyne

56: **COMMUNICATION BASICS FOR HUMAN SERVICE PROFESSIONALS** by Elam Nunnally and Caryl Moy

57: **COMMUNICATION DISORDERS IN AGING** edited by Raymond H. Hull and Kathleen M. Griffin

58: **THE PRACTICE OF CASE MANAGEMENT** by David P. Moxley

59: **MEASUREMENT IN DIRECT PRACTICE** by Betty J. Blythe and Tony Tripodi

60: **BUILDING COALITIONS IN THE HUMAN SERVICES** by Milan J. Dluhy with the assistance of Sanford L. Kravitz

61: **PSYCHIATRIC MEDICATIONS** by Kenneth J. Bender

62: **PRACTICE WISDOM** by Donald F. Krill

63: **PROPOSAL WRITING** by Soraya M. Coley and Cynthia A. Scheinberg

64: **QUALITY ASSURANCE FOR LONG-TERM CARE PROVIDERS** by William Ammentorp, Kenneth D. Gossett, and Nancy Euchner Poe

65: **GROUP COUNSELING WITH JUVENILE DELINQUENTS** by Matthew L. Ferrara

66: **ADVANCED CASE MANAGEMENT: New Strategies for the Nineties** by Norma Radol Raiff and Barbara Shore

67: **TOTAL QUALITY MANAGEMENT IN HUMAN SERVICE ORGANIZATIONS** by Lawrence L. Martin

68: **CONDUCTING NEEDS ASSESSMENTS** by Fernando I. Soriano

69: **ORAL HISTORY IN SOCIAL WORK** by Ruth R. Martin

70: **THE FIRST HELPING INTERVIEW: Engaging the Client and Building Trust** by Sara F. Fine and Paul H. Glasser

71: **MEASURING THE PERFORMANCE OF HUMAN SERVICE PROGRAMS** by Lawrence L. Martin and Peter M. Kettner (second edition)

72: **CREATING SMALL SCALE SOCIAL PROGRAMS: Planning, Implementation, and Evaluation** by Barbara Schram

73: **GOAL-FOCUSED INTERVIEWING** by Frank F. Maple

74: **IMPROVING ORGANIZATIONAL PERFORMANCE: A Practical Guidebook for the Human Services Field** by Gary V. Sluyter

Second Edition
Measuring the
Performance of
Human Service
Programs

LAWRENCE L. MARTIN
University of Central Florida

PETER M. KETTNER
Arizona State University

Los Angeles | London | New Delhi
Singapore | Washington DC

For information:

SAGE Publications, Inc.
2455 Teller Road
Thousand Oaks,
  California 91320
E-mail: order@sagepub.com

SAGE Publications India Pvt. Ltd.
B 1/I 1 Mohan Cooperative
  Industrial Area
Mathura Road, New Delhi 110 044
India

SAGE Publications Ltd.
1 Oliver's Yard
55 City Road
London EC1Y 1SP
United Kingdom

SAGE Publications Asia-Pacific Pte. Ltd.
33 Pekin Street #02-01
Far East Square
Singapore 048763

Printed in the United States of America

Library of Congress Cataloging-in-Publication Data

Martin, Lawrence L.
Measuring the performance of human service programs/Lawrence L. Martin and Peter M. Kettner. — 2nd ed.
    p. cm.
(Sage Human Services Guides ; v. 71)
Includes bibliographical references and index.
ISBN 978-1-4129-7061-7 (pbk.)
    1. Human services—Evaluation—Methodology. 2. Evaluation research (Social action programs) 3. Present value analysis. I. Kettner, Peter M., 1936– II. Title.

HV11.M3494 2010
362.068′4—dc22   2008055823

This book is printed on acid-free paper.

09   10   11   12   13   10   9   8   7   6   5   4   3   2   1

Acquisitions Editor:	Kassie Graves
Editorial Assistant:	Veronica K. Novak
Production Editor:	Brittany Bauhaus
Copy Editor:	Teresa Wilson
Typesetter:	C&M Digitals (P) Ltd.
Proofreader:	Theresa Kay
Indexer:	Rick Hurd
Cover Designer:	Bryan Fishman
Marketing Manager:	Carmel Schrire

Contents

Preface   ix
   Acknowledgments   x

1. Performance Accountability and
Performance Measurement   1
   Introduction   1
   What Is a Program?   3
   What Is Performance Measurement?   4
   Performance Measurement and the Systems Model   4
      The Efficiency Perspective   6
      The Quality Perspective   7
      The Effectiveness Perspective   8
   Why Adopt Performance Measurement?   9
      Performance Measurement and Improved
         Program Management 9
      Performance Measurement and
         Resource Allocation Decisions 10
      Performance Measurement as a Forced Choice 11

2. Putting Performance Accountability and
Performance Measurement in Perspective   13
   Introduction   13
   The Forces Promoting Performance
      Accountability and Performance Measurement 14
      Government Performance and Results Act 14
      Service Efforts and Accomplishments Reporting 16
      Total Quality Management Approach   16
      The Outcomes Movement in the Human Services 17
      Performance-Based Payment Mechanisms 18
   The Language and Structure of SEA Reporting   19
      Service Efforts   19

Service Accomplishments   21
Service Efforts and Accomplishments Ratios   22
Developing and Using Performance Measures   23

**3. Logic Models, Human Service Programs,
and Performance Measurement**   **25**
Introduction   25
Developing a Logic Model   27
Task 1: Specify the Agency,
Community, or Social Problem   28
Task 2: Identify the Program Assumptions   29
Task 3: Design the Program   30
Agency Strategic Plan Focus   32
Community Problem or Need Focus   34
Social Problem Focus   34

4. Output Performance Measures   **39**
Introduction   39
What Are Output Performance Measures?   40
Developing Intermediate Output Performance Measures   41
Definition of Unit of Service   41
Types of Units of Service   42
Selecting a Unit of Service   43
Units of Service and Programs of Services   45
Final Output Performance Measures   47
Defining a Service Completion   47
Developing Service Completions   48
Service Completions and Client Outcomes   50

5. Quality Performance Measures   **51**
Introduction   51
What Is Quality?   52
The Dimensions of Quality   52
Types of Quality Performance Measures   55
Outputs With Quality Dimensions Approach   56
Client Satisfaction Approach   58

6. Outcome Performance Measures   **63**
Introduction   63
What Are Outcome Performance Measures?   63
Client Problems Versus Client End States   64
The Four Types of Outcome Performance Measures   66

Intermediate and Final Outcome Performance Measures   67

Selecting Outcome Performance Measures   68

     Step 1: Convene Stakeholder Focus Group   69

     Step 2: Assess Outcome Performance Measures   69

     Step 3: Select Outcome Performance Measures   69

Cause-and-Effect Relationships   69

Social Indicators as Final Outcome Performance Measures   71

Outcome Performance Measures and Programs of Services   75

Assessing the Four Types

     of Outcome Performance Measures   76

7. Numeric Counts   **79**

Introduction   79

What Are Numeric Counts?   79

Examples of Numeric Counts   80

The Preference for Numeric Counts   84

An Assessment of Numeric Counts   84

8. Standardized Measures   **87**

Introduction   87

What Are Standardized Measures?   87

The Use of Standardized Measures

     for Evaluation Versus Research   88

Differences in Standardized Measures   90

     Concept Measured   90

     Structure of Scale   91

     Type of Respondent   92

     Availability of a Clinical Cutting Score   92

     Validity and Reliability   92

     Time, Effort, and Training Needed to Administer   93

Locating Standardized Measures   93

Using Standardized Measures as

     Outcome Performance Measures   94

Translating Standardized Measures Into Numeric Counts   95

An Assessment of Standardized Measures   96

9. Level of Functioning (LOF) Scales   **99**

Introduction   99

What Are Level of Functioning (LOF) Scales?   100

Principles in Designing LOF Scales   100

     Developing a Conceptual Framework   101

     Developing Descriptors   102

Respondent Family Considerations 105
Constructing LOF Scales 108
Translating LOF Scales Into Numeric Counts 110
An Assessment of LOF Scales 111

10. Client Satisfaction **113**
Introduction 113
Using Client Satisfaction as an
  Outcome Performance Measure 113
Translating Client Satisfaction
  Outcomes Into Numeric Counts 115
An Assessment of Client Satisfaction 115
An Assessment of the Four Types
  of Outcome Performance Measures 117

11. Using Performance Measurement Information **119**
Introduction 119
The Town 119
The Agency and the Human Service Programs 120
Planning Using Performance Measures 121
    Developing Performance Measures and Objectives 121
Monitoring Performance 123
Reporting Using Performance Measures 126
Performance Accountability and Performance
  Measurement 129

References **131**

Index **137**

About the Authors **147**

Preface

Much has changed in terms of performance accountability and performance measurement in human service programs since the first edition of this text appeared in 1996. What was then an emerging concept has evolved into a basic approach to how human service programs are conceptualized, implemented, and evaluated. Today, mastering the subject matter of performance accountability and performance measurement is no longer just a nice idea but is an essential skill for all human service professionals.

In this second edition, the goal of the authors is to bring the subject matter and literature of performance accountability and performance measurement up-to-date while maintaining the conciseness and readability of the first edition. The original text remains unchanged where the concepts and issues are still relevant and has been updated wherever they have changed. This second edition continues to utilize the three-pronged approach (outputs, quality, and outcomes) to performance accountability and performance measurement. Individual chapters continue to be devoted to detailed discussions of the purposes of each of these three types of performance measures and their applications.

New to this edition is the inclusion of additional detail on the development of outcome performance measures (numeric counts, standardized measures, level of functioning [LOF] scales, and client satisfaction). A new Chapter 3 illustrates the use of logic models in the development of performance measures for human service programs. A revised Chapter 11 includes an expanded discussion of the use of performance measurement information (including "dashboards") to monitor human service program implementation.

For educators, we would like to point out that a CD is available from SAGE that includes suggested assignments as well as PowerPoint slides for each chapter. To obtain a copy of this CD, please contact SAGE Customer Care at 1-800-818-SAGE (7243), 6am–5pm PT.

Acknowledgments

The authors would like to thank Ms. Kassie Graves, SAGE Acquisitions Editor for Human Services, for encouraging us to undertake this second edition, and Ms. Veronica Novak, Senior Editorial Assistant, for her assistance in preparing the manuscript for publication.

The authors and SAGE gratefully acknowledge the contributions of the following reviewers:

Dr. Shirley E. Cox, *Brigham Young University*

Diane DePanfilis, *University of Maryland, School of Social Work*

Rob Fischer, *Case Western Reserve University*

Catalina Herrerías, *University of Oklahoma*

Mark Krain, *University of Arkansas at Little Rock*

Jennifer Magnabosco, *UCLA/Loyola Marymount*

Steven Rose, *George Mason University*

Elizabeth A. Segal, *Arizona State University*

Yvonne A. Unrau, *Western Michigan University*

—*Lawrence L. Martin*
—*Peter M. Kettner*

One

Performance Accountability and Performance Measurement

Introduction

Performance accountability and performance measurement are important elements of how human service organizations plan, resource, manage, and assess their programs. Performance accountability provides the theoretical framework, while performance measurement deals with the "how-to." Human service managers today need to understand both the theory and the how-to in order to successfully operate in an environment dominated by concerns with performance accountability and performance measurement.

Performance accountability and performance measurement apply not only to human service programs, but to most programs operated by the federal government, state and local governments, the United Way, and foundations. Programs operated by nonprofit organizations are also affected by performance accountability and performance

1

measurement because most of these organizations receive funding from governments, the United Way, or foundations (Martin, 2001, 2005; Zimmerman & Stevens, 2006).

Historically, human service programs were primarily concerned with *process* issues (Kettner, Moroney, & Martin, 2008; McDavid & Hawthorn, 2006; Rossi, Lipsey, & Freeman, 2004). Was the program implemented as designed? Did the program reach its target population? Were subgroups (e.g., ethnic populations, persons with disabilities, women, seniors, etc.) served in appropriate proportions? Was the geographical coverage adequate? Were the program expenditures appropriate? (And other process type considerations.) If all process considerations were satisfied, then the program was considered successful. As long as human service programs were meeting a need and exercising proper stewardship over their funds, questions of performance (what results were achieved?) were seldom raised. Human service programs were assumed to have intrinsic value. This situation began to change in the early 1990s (Bliss, 2007; Mulvaney, Zwahr, & Baranowski, 2006).

Today, it is not enough for human service programs to demonstrate process accountability; they need to demonstrate *performance* accountability. It is performance that matters, and issues of process are relegated to a secondary status. In commenting upon performance accountability, the president of the United Way of America has stated that those organizations that understand and adopt performance accountability "will strengthen their reputations and increase their competitive standing. Those that fail to do so risk their very existence" (Gallagher, 2008).

The transition from a process orientation to a performance orientation has been particularly difficult for the human services and for human service professionals. Because so many human service programs involve professional interactions between staff and clients, process concerns have historically dominated thinking and practice. The initial response of the human services to the performance accountability movement was, "You can't measure what we do!" (e.g., American Public Welfare Association [APWA], 1980; R. Millar & Millar, 1981). Setting aside the argument of whether this was true in the past, it is clearly not an acceptable argument today. Regardless of the type of human service program in question, some agency somewhere today is already measuring its performance.

What Is a Program?

Before proceeding further, it is useful to pause and consider the issue: What is a program? Being clear about what constitutes a program is important because performance accountability and performance measurement are based on "program" as the unit of analysis. Since the human services have dealt with programs for a long time, one would assume that common agreement exists on what constitutes a program. Unfortunately, this is not the case! No universally agreed upon definition of a program exists (Gilmour, 2006; Martin, 2008). Throughout this book, the following definition of *program* (Martin, 2008) will be utilized:

> A program is a major ongoing agency activity or service with its own sets of policies, goals, objectives, and budgets that produces a defined product or service.

As the definition makes explicit, a program is a major ongoing agency activity or service. For performance accountability and performance measurement purposes, not everything a human service agency does should be treated as a program. A program is one of the important few ongoing activities or services provided by a human service agency. A program can be further differentiated from other agency activities by the presence of its own policies, goals, objectives, and budgets. The acid test for a program is said to be if it has its own budget (e.g., Smith & Lynch, 2004).

Finally, a program produces a defined product or service. For example, a home-delivered meals program produces meals; a counseling program produces hours of counseling; and a specialized transportation program produces trips.

The question is frequently raised: Can performance accountability and performance measurement principles be applied to entire human service agencies rather than just to programs? The answer to this question is a qualified "Yes." The basic concepts of performance accountability and performance measurement can be, and have been, applied to agencies, communities, states, and even to whole countries. However, for purposes of this book, the focus remains on "program" as the unit of analysis.

Having defined what a program is, attention is now directed to a discussion of what performance measurement is.

What Is Performance Measurement?

Performance measurement can be defined as the following:

> The regular collection and reporting of information about the *efficiency*, *quality*, and *effectiveness* of programs.

This definition has been around for many years (Urban Institute, 1980) and has withstood the test of time. Most of the major government performance accountability and performance measurement systems today are based upon this definition.

Performance measurement, as the concept is generally understood (e.g., Carmeli, 2006; E. Fischer, 2005; Mulvaney et al., 2006; Zimmerman & Stevens, 2006), is comprised of the three dimensions of *efficiency*, *quality*, and *effectiveness*. This multidimensional approach enables performance information and data on human service programs to be viewed from different perspectives by different stakeholders with different opinions about the nature of performance accountability (Martin, 2002; Rossi et al., 2004). Performance measurement implies no hierarchy or preference among these three perspectives, but rather assumes that all three are important to at least some stakeholders.

Performance Measurement and the Systems Model

In discussing performance measurement, it is useful to refer to what we call the "expanded systems model" (Kettner et al., 2008; Martin, 2002). The basic systems model (Figure 1.1) has long been used as an aid in understanding how human service programs operate (e.g., Ables & Murphy, 1981; Rosenberg & Brody, 1974). The core elements of the basic systems model are *inputs, process, outputs,* and *feedback.* The expanded systems model (Figure 1.2) brings the basic systems model up to date by adding two more components: *quality* and *outcomes.*

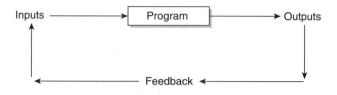

Figure 1.1   The Basic Systems Model

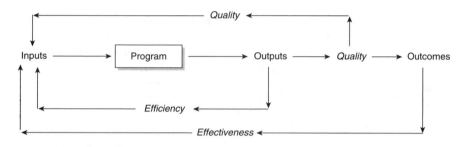

Figure 1.2   The Expanded Systems Model

- *Inputs* are anything a system (a human service program) uses to accomplish its purposes. More specifically, inputs can be thought of as the resources and raw materials (e.g., funding, staff, facilities, equipment, clients, presenting problems, etc.) that go into a human service program.
- *Process* constitutes the treatment plan or service delivery methodology (a human service program) during which inputs are consumed and translated into outputs.
- *Outputs* are anything a system (a human service program) produces. In human service programs, outputs are also frequently referred to as *units of service*.
- *Quality* is measured in terms of those dimensions (e.g., timeliness, empathy, responsiveness, humaneness, etc.) that are most important to the stakeholders of a human service program.
- *Outcomes* are the results, accomplishments, or impacts achieved, at least partially, by a human service program.
- *Feedback* can be thought of as data and information about the performance of a system (a human service program) that is reintroduced into the system as an additional input.

The system elements of inputs, process, outputs, quality, outcomes, and feedback can be utilized to explain the three accountability perspectives of efficiency, quality, and effectiveness.

Table 1.1   The Three Dimensions of Performance Accountability and Performance Measurement

Dimension of performance	Definition	Example
Efficiency	The ratio of outputs to inputs	The total costs of a foster care program divided by the number of foster care days of service
Quality	The number or proportion of outputs that meet a quality standard	The number or percentage of home-delivered meals that arrive hot
Effectiveness	The ratio of outcomes to inputs	The total costs of an adoptions program divided by the number of finalized adoptions achieved

Table 1.1 shows the operational definitions of the terms *efficiency, quality,* and *effectiveness* that are utilized throughout this book.

The Efficiency Perspective

Performance accountability and performance measurement include a focus on efficiency. From the efficiency perspective, the primary performance focus for a human service program is on outputs and the comparison of outputs to inputs. For example, in looking at a human service program from the efficiency perspective, one assesses the amount of service provided (outputs) and compares the number of outputs to the costs involved (inputs).

The ratio of outputs to inputs is the classical definition of productivity. Accordingly, feedback on the performance of a human service program (Figure 1.2) takes the form of tracking and reporting on outputs. An accountable human service program, according to the efficiency perspective of performance accountability, is one that strives to maximize outputs in relation to inputs.

The efficiency perspective of performance accountability has a history of neglect in the human services (e.g., Pruger & Miller, 1991). All too frequently, efficiency has been used as a rationale for funding cuts and—in some instances—for outright attacks on the legitimacy of human service programs. Many human service administrators view a focus on efficiency as misguided, all too frequently resulting in goal displacement. "You can do the wrong thing very efficiently" is a criticism frequently vocalized.

Despite the criticisms made of the efficiency perspective of performance accountability, several good reasons exist why it should be a major focus of human service programs:

1. The requirements of public stewardship demand that every dollar spent on human service programs be put to the best possible use to ensure that as many eligible clients as possible are served.

2. Efficiency or productivity considerations are a basic operating assumption of most fee-for-service contracts, performance-based contracts, managed care programs, and other funding strategies.

3. A high-profile position supporting efficiency or productivity is necessary to counter the image held by at least some stakeholders that human service programs are inefficient. Only some 11% of Americans today believe that human service agencies do a very good job of spending money wisely (Gallagher, 2008).

The Quality Perspective

A performance focus on service quality accountability differs from that of the efficiency perspective. Throughout the 1980s and continuing today, the writings of the top quality management gurus (e.g., Crosby, 1985; Deming, 1986; Juran, 1989) have had a major impact on management thinking and practices in the United States and around the world. Today, most publicly funded programs, including human service programs, are expected to routinely assess the quality of their services and to "benchmark"— or compare—their results with other programs operated by other public and private agencies.

The quality management movement has influenced the classical definition of productivity to include quality considerations. According to quality management theory, productivity is increased when programs provide high-quality services and is decreased when low-quality services are provided (e.g., Gunther & Hawkins, 1996; Martin, 1993a). For human service programs, the implication of this expanded definition of productivity is that high-quality services should result in lower error rates, less paperwork, less reprocessing time, happier funding sources, more satisfied clients, lower costs, and a better public image.

The quality perspective to performance accountability actually changes the definition of productivity to the ratio of *outputs that meet a specified quality standard* to inputs. For example, the proportion of meals in a home-delivered meals program that arrive hot or the proportion of trips in a specialized transportation program that arrive at their destinations on time are examples of outputs that meet a quality standard. Feedback on the performance of human service programs necessarily takes the form of tracking and reporting on the number of outputs that meet a quality standard. An accountable human service program according to the quality perspective (Figure 1.2) is one that strives to maximize quality outputs in relation to inputs.

The Effectiveness Perspective

From the effectiveness perspective, performance accountability incorporates a focus on outcomes (the results, accomplishments, or impacts) of human service programs (Governmental Accounting Standards Board [GASB], 1993, 2008). Examples of outcomes include the number of adoptions achieved by an adoptions program, the number of parents who stop abusing and neglecting their children following completion of a parental skills training program, or the number of juvenile offenders who have no further encounters with the juvenile justice system as a result of an intensive case management program. Effectiveness is often considered the highest form of performance accountability.

Unlike traditional program evaluation, performance measurement is not concerned with one-shot assessments of results, accomplishments, or impacts. Instead, performance measurement belongs to the school of thought that holds that human service programs cannot be divorced from their social settings (Cronbach, 1982). Consequently, performance measurement is less concerned with attempting to demonstrate scientifically defensible cause-and-effect relationships (Rocheleau, 1988) and is more concerned with basic practice questions such as what outcomes are achieved by what types of human service programs (Kettner et al., 2008). Performance measurement enables judgments to be made about the effectiveness of human service programs during implementation as well as after, thus capturing both the *formative* and *summative* approaches to program evaluation (Rossi et al., 2004).

Effectiveness accountability is concerned with the ratio of outcomes to inputs. Accordingly, feedback on the performance of human service programs takes the form of tracking and reporting on outcomes. According to the effectiveness perspective (Figure 1.2), an accountable human service program is one that strives to maximize outcomes in relation to inputs.

When compared to each other (Figure 1.2), it is apparent that the efficiency, quality, and effectiveness perspectives to human service program accountability are distinctive. Not only do these three perspectives conceptualize program performance accountability differently, but they also emphasize different types of feedback. Because performance measurement draws on all three perspectives, it creates one comprehensive approach to performance accountability.

Why Adopt Performance Measurement?

Why should human service administrators adopt performance accountability and performance measurement? In addition to accountability reporting, are there other important factors to consider? Proponents of performance measurement point out at least three:

1. Performance accountability and performance measurement have the potential to improve the management of human service programs.

2. Performance accountability and performance measurement have the potential to affect the allocation of resources among human service programs and non-human service programs.

3. Performance accountability and performance measurement may well be a forced choice for most human service programs. Funding sources, both governmental and nongovernmental, are increasingly adopting performance accountability and performance measurement. In some instances, funding sources may prescribe the use of specific performance measures as a precondition to receiving contracts and grants.

Performance Measurement and Improved Program Management

To properly manage their human service programs, administrators must be clear about the following questions:

- Who are their clients?
- What are their demographic characteristics?
- What are their social or presenting problems?

- What services are they receiving?
- In what amounts?
- What is the level of service quality?
- What results, accomplishments, or impacts are being achieved?
- What is the total cost?

Most human service programs are relatively clear about the answers to the first four questions. Some are frequently unclear about the latter four. And a few are not even sure what the questions are. For the most part, the inability of human service programs to answer all eight questions is due largely to the absence of formally adopted measures of efficiency, quality, and effectiveness.

Performance accountability and performance measurement provide the missing pieces that can enable human service administrators to answer all eight questions about their programs. Combining performance measurement data with client and problem data provides human service administrators with the ability to identify which programs achieve what results with what types of clients and at what costs. Armed with this type of information, human service administrators should be able to plan, design, and implement more efficient, more effective, and better quality programs.

If the above arguments are not sufficient, performance accountability and performance measurement have still other features that make them a valuable management tool for human service administrators. As will be demonstrated in this book, performance accountability and performance measurement

1. promote client centeredness by making client outcomes a central component of program performance;

2. provide a common language that human service administrators can use to make evaluative judgments about the efficiency, quality, and effectiveness of the programs they manage;

3. enable human service administrators to continually monitor their programs to identify "points of intervention" for service improvements; and

4. improve the morale of direct service workers who get feedback on what clients are being helped and by how much.

Performance Measurement and Resource Allocation Decisions

Performance measurement also has the potential to significantly affect the resource allocation decisions of governmental and nongovernmental organizations. If all human service programs were to collect and report comparable performance measures, then government and private funding sources could use the resulting data and information to make budgeting, grant, and contracting decisions.

What is the purpose, some might ask, of collecting information on the performance of human service programs if the data are not then used to reward those that perform and to penalize those that do not? For example, let's assume there are two human service agencies (X and Y), both of which operate in the same community, operate the same program, and receive the majority of their funding from the United Way. Agency X provides more service (outputs) and gets better results with clients (outcomes) for less money than Agency Y. *Agency X then should receive more funding and Agency Y less funding.*

Performance accountability and performance measurement are not restricted to just human service programs, but extend to all government-funded programs. Consequently, performance measurement—carried to its logical conclusion—could become an important factor not only in making resource allocation decisions between competing human service programs but also in making resource allocation decisions between the human services and other competing societal needs such as health care, housing, education infrastructure, and others.

Performance Measurement as a Forced Choice

Although some human service administrators might prefer to ignore the opportunity to adopt performance measurement, they may have little choice in the matter. Most human service funding sources (government, United Way, foundations) require some sort of performance measurement on the part of human service programs as a condition to receiving funding (e.g., Bliss, 2007; E. Fischer, 2005). Chapter 2 discusses more fully the forces promoting performance accountability and performance measurement.

Two

Putting Performance Accountability and Performance Measurement in Perspective

Introduction

Most major funding sources have made performance accountability and performance measurement an integral part of their basic management systems. The increased use of performance accountability and performance measurement is the result of several forces, including federal and state laws and regulations, total quality management principles, the outcomes movement in the human services, and performance-based payment mechanisms.

In this chapter, the major forces promoting performance accountability and performance measurement are first presented and discussed. Next, the service efforts and accomplishments (SEA) reporting initiative of the Governmental Accounting Standards Board (GASB) is introduced and discussed. The language and structure of SEA reporting is used as an organizing framework throughout this book.

The Forces Promoting Performance Accountability and Performance Measurement

The general acceptance of performance accountability and performance measurement is the result of several forces, some stretching back to the early 1990s, while others are more recent. Some of these forces are primarily governmental (federal, state, or local), but they also have implications for nonprofits and for-profits. Other forces represent private sector initiatives (e.g., United Way of America and foundations). Still other forces are directed at selected government human service programs. Individually, each of these forces is important by itself. Combined (Table 2.1), these forces virtually ensure that all human service agencies and programs will eventually be required to adopt performance accountability and performance measurement.

Government Performance and Results Act

Probably the most important of all the major forces promoting performance accountability and performance measurement is the Government Performance and Results Act (GPRA, 1993). GPRA is a federal law passed by Congress in 1993. GPRA requires that every program operated by every federal department and agency annually report to the president and the Congress on its performance. The passage of GPRA represents a major milestone in the history of performance accountability and performance measurement. GPRA established the principle that the unit of analysis would be the program and that henceforth performance accountability and performance measurement would be the major method by which federal programs would be assessed.

GPRA states a clear preference for the *effectiveness* (outcome) perspective to performance accountability and performance measurement, which it defines as the "results, accomplishments or impacts" of federal programs. GPRA's preference for the effectiveness (outcome) perspective has been further emphasized by the federal Office of Management and Budget (OMB), the organization charged with overseeing implementation and reporting on the act (Gilmour, 2006). Despite its preference for the effectiveness (outcome) perspective, GPRA also clearly recognizes the importance of the efficiency (outputs) perspective as well as the quality

Table 2.1   The Major Forces Promoting Performance Accountability and
Performance Measurement

Major force	Approximate year(s)	What it does
Government Performance and Results Act (GPRA)	1993	Requires all federal departments and agencies to report annually on the performance of their programs
Governmental Accounting Standards Board (GASB) service efforts and accomplishments (SEA) reporting	1993, 2008	Establishes a framework for performance accountability and performance measurement for state and local governments
Total quality management (TQM) movement	1980s, 1990s	Promotes the use of quality performance measures
Outcomes movement in the human services	1990s, 2000s	Places emphasis on the creation, use, and reporting of outcomes
Performance-based payment mechanisms	1990s, 2000s	Links performance to funding

perspective. Consequently, GPRA also firmly establishes the principle that performance accountability and performance measurement are multidimensional.

GPRA *directly* affects all federal departments and agencies, but it also *indirectly* affects state and local governments, for-profits, and nonprofits. Most federal programs are implemented through grants and contracts. Consequently, the only way federal programs can meet the mandates of GPRA is to require their grantees and contractors (state and local governments, for-profits, and nonprofits) to also report performance measurement data.

Service Efforts and Accomplishments Reporting

The Governmental Accounting Standards Board (GASB) is the organization that establishes "generally accepted accounting principles" for state and local governments. For state and local governments to receive unqualified opinions (no exceptions noted) on their financial reports and audits from certified public accountants and auditors, all GASB standards must be met.

In 1993, the same year that GPRA came into being, GASB launched an initiative it calls "service efforts and accomplishments (SEA) reporting" (GASB, 1993). SEA reporting does for state and local governments what GPRA did for the federal government: It establishes a framework for performance accountability and performance measurement. Just like GPRA, SEA reporting adopts the program as the unit of analysis and identifies three dimensions of performance: efficiency, quality, and effectiveness. Unlike GPRA, however, SEA reporting does not single out effectiveness for special emphasis. Rather, SEA reporting suggests that all three dimensions of performance are equally important. SEA reporting is not directed specifically at human service programs, but at all state and local government-funded programs.

To date, GASB has only recommended, not mandated, that state and local governments adopt SEA reporting (GASB, 2008). Nevertheless, most state governments and numerous local governments (counties, cities, and towns) have adopted some form of performance accountability and performance measurement based on the SEA reporting framework (Melkers & Willoughby, 1998). Since many state and local government programs and services themselves are actually provided under grants, contracts, and other third-party arrangements, SEA reporting also indirectly affects nonprofit and for-profit organizations. Because of the important intermediate position between the federal government and nonprofits and for-profits played by state and local governments and because of its comprehensive nature, the SEA reporting framework is utilized throughout this book.

Total Quality Management Approach

Total quality management (TQM) is both a response to and a force promoting performance accountability and performance measurement. In addition to making human service administrators more conscious about promoting quality in their programs, the TQM movement has also affected the nature of performance accountability and performance measurement.

Quality performance measures are now routinely included together with the more traditional efficiency and effectiveness performance measures (Bliss, 2007; Kettner, Moroney, & Martin, 2008). For example, the Council on Accreditation (2008) includes "leadership endorsement of quality and performance values" as part of its standards for both public and private organizations.

Quality performance measures generally take one of two forms: (a) consumer (client) satisfaction or (b) outputs that meet a specified quality standard (Martin, 1993b). An example of the first approach might be the proportion of clients in a specialized transportation program who rate the quality of the service as either *very good* or *excellent*. Examples of the second approach might include (a) the proportion of meals in a home-delivered meals program that arrive hot and (b) the proportion of graduates in a job training program that possess marketable job skills upon completion of their training. Quality performance measures are discussed more completely in Chapter 5.

The Outcomes Movement in the Human Services

Perhaps no other topic in the human services receives more attention today than that of outcomes and outcome measurement. Outcomes and outcome performance measures are arguably the highest form of performance accountability. The outcomes movement can be traced back to GPRA and its preference for outcome performance accountability and performance measurement. But it may well be the outcome measurement initiatives of the United Way of America and other national human service organizations (e.g., American Red Cross, Goodwill Industries, Lutheran Services in America, Alliance for Children and Families, and others) that are responsible for many nonprofits having their first close encounter with performance accountability and performance measurement (United Way of America, 1996a, 1996b, 2003).

With all levels of government, as well as the United Way of America, advocating the adoption of outcomes and outcome performance measures, it was perhaps only a matter of time before foundations and other funding sources began doing the same. Today, the requirement to collect and report performance measurement data with an emphasis on outcomes is simply a basic part of the administration of human service programs (E. Fisher, 2005).

Some examples of the way in which the outcomes movement has taken hold in the human services are provided by the Adoption and Safe Families Act (1997) and the Workforce Investment Act (1998). Both of these programs mandate specific outcome performance measures (Table 2.2). State and local governments as well as nonprofits and for-profits that receive funding under either of these two federal programs are required to collect and report data and information on the specified outcome performance measures.

Performance-Based Payment Mechanisms

Governments (federal, state, and local) as well as some United Ways and foundations now routinely link performance and funding through performance-based budgeting, grants, and contracts (Martin, 2005; Melkers & Willoughby, 1998; Smith & Lynch, 2004). The federal government's contracting regulations, the Federal Acquisition Regulation (FAR), require that performance-based contracting be utilized to the

Table 2.2   Outcome Performance Measures Included in the Adoption and Safe Families Act and the Workforce Investment Act

Adoption and Safe Families Act Outcome Measures*
1. Reduction in recurrence of child abuse and/or neglect
2. Decrease in time spent in foster care
3. Increase in permanency for children in foster care
4. Increased permanency stability
Source: U.S. Department of Health and Human Services (2008).
Workforce Investment Act Outcome Measures*
1. Entry into unsubsidized employment
2. Retention in unsubsidized employment for six months
3. Earnings in unsubsidized employment after six months
4. Attainment of a recognized credential relating to achievement of educational skills
Source: U.S. Department of Labor (2008).
*Partial Listing

"maximum extent practicable." Many states (Arizona, Florida, Illinois, Indiana, Maine, North Carolina, Oklahoma, and others) require the use of performance-based contracting for some or all human service programs (Martin, 2005, 2007). Under the terms of many performance-based contracts and grants, human service agencies and programs only receive funding when they accomplish specific efficiency (output), quality, and effectiveness (outcome) performance measures (Martin, 2007).

As Figure 2.1 illustrates, the major forces promoting performance accountability and performance measurement combine to create a "performance environment" that provides a context and a framework that makes performance measurement feasibile, useful, and inevitable.

The Language and Structure of SEA Reporting

SEA reporting (Table 2.3) can be divided into three elements: (1) service efforts, (2) service accomplishments, and (3) measures, or ratios, that relate service efforts to service accomplishments (GASB, 1993, 2008).

Service Efforts

Service efforts are the resources (inputs) that go into a human service program. SEA reporting measures service efforts in three ways: (a) the total cost of a program, (b) the total full-time equivalent (FTE) positions

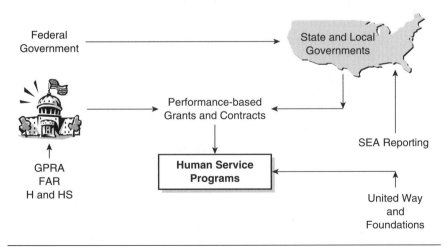

Figure 2.1   The Performance Environment

Table 2.3   The Elements of Service Efforts and Accomplishments Reporting

I. Service efforts

A. Financial information

   1. Total cost measured in dollars

B. Nonfinancial information

   1. Number of personnel: the total number of full-time equivalent (FTE) positions

   2. Other measures (e.g., the total number of employee hours expended)

II. Service accomplishments

A. Outputs

   1. Total volume of service provided

B. Quality

   1. The number (#) or proportion (%) of the total service volume that meets a specified quality standard

C. Outcomes

   1. Measures of the results, accomplishments, or impacts achieved (partially or totally)

III. Service efforts and accomplishments ratios

A. Efficiency measures

   1. The ratio of service volume (outputs) to resources consumed (inputs) as measured by

      a. Cost per output

      b. Outputs per FTE

      c. Outputs per hour worked

B. Effectiveness measures

   1. The ratio of results, accomplishments, or impacts (outcomes) to resources consumed (inputs) as measured by

      a. Cost per outcome

      b. Outcomes per FTE

      c. Outcomes per hour worked

devoted to a program, and (c) the total number of employee hours worked on a program. SEA reporting assumes that human service agencies operating multiple programs have already adopted, or have the capability to adopt, program budgeting. The importance of this assumption should not be overlooked. The performance cost ratios (cost per output and cost per outcome) cannot be determined if a human service agency has not defined its program structure or lacks a method for allocating organizational overhead or indirect costs to its programs (Martin, 2001). Table 2.4 is a hypothetical example of a fiscal year service efforts report for a family counseling program providing intensive training and counseling to abusive and/or neglecting parents.

Service Accomplishments

Service accomplishments are divided into two main categories: (a) *outputs* and (b) *outcomes*. Outputs are further subdivided into (a) *outputs* (which capture the efficiency perspective of performance accountability) and (b) *outputs that meet a specified quality standard* (which capture the quality perspective of performance accountability). *Outcomes* capture the effectiveness perspective of performance accountability. It should be made clear that SEA reporting is concerned with establishing a framework for performance accountability and performance measurement and not with mandating specific performance measures for specific programs.

Table 2.5 is an example of what a fiscal year service accomplishments report might look like for the sample family counseling program.

Table 2.4   Service Efforts and Accomplishments Input Elements

Service efforts	Example
1. Total cost	$750,000
2. FTEs	22
3. Hours worked	45,760*

*Based on a 2,080 hour (52 weeks × 40 hours per week) work year for 22 employees

Table 2.5   Service Efforts and Accomplishments Performance Elements

Service accomplishments	Examples
1. Outputs – The quantity of service provided measured in units of service – The quantity of service provided measured in terms of service completions*	27,500 hours of parent training and counseling are provided. 225 parents complete the program.
2. Quality – The quantity of service provided that meets a specified quality standard	At least 85% of completing parents (n = 191) rate the service as *very helpful* or *helpful*.
3. Outcomes – The results, accomplishments, or impacts of service	At least 112 parents will have no reports of abuse or neglect for a minimum of 2 years following completion of the program.

*A service completion equals one client completing treatment or receiving a full complement of services.

Service Efforts and Accomplishments Ratios

The computation of specific ratios is the third element in SEA reporting. These ratios relate service efforts to service accomplishments through such measures as

1. cost per unit of service (output or outcome),

2. units of service (output or outcome) per FTE (full-time equivalent) position, and

3. units of service (output or outcome) per hour worked.

Table 2.6 presents some examples of what SEA ratios might look like for the sample family counseling program. As can be seen, the SEA ratios provide a variety of ways of assessing accountability in the family counseling agency. There is something for every stakeholder. Some measures may be of more interest to citizens, elected officials, and advocacy groups; others to government funding agencies, accountants, and auditors; and still others to clients, board members, agency administrators, or caseworkers.

Table 2.6   Service Efforts and Accomplishments Ratios

SEA ratios	*Example*
1. Efficiency (output) measures	
a. Cost per unit of service	$27.27 ($750,000/27,500)
b. Units of service per FTE	1,250 (27,500/22 FTE staff)
c. Cost per service completion	$3,333 ($750,000/225)
d. Service completions per FTE	10.23 (225/22)
2. Effectiveness (outcome) measures	
a. Cost per outcome	$6,696.42 ($750,000/112)
b. Outcomes per FTE	5.01 (112/22)
3. Interpretations	
a. The average cost per hour of training is $27.27.	
b. Each trainer provided an average of 1,250 hours of training.	
c. The average cost per family completing the training was $3,333.	
d. Each trainer resulted in 10.23 families completing the training.	
e. The cost to achieve the outcome of one family not abusing or neglecting its children for a minimum period of 2 years is $6,696.42.	
f. The average number of outcomes attributable to each trainer is 5.01.	

Developing and Using Performance Measures

In subsequent chapters, the development and use of performance measures based on the SEA reporting format are discussed in depth, including outputs, quality, and outcomes. Table 2.7 provides an overview of the categories and types of performance measures to be discussed.

As Table 2.7 illustrates, the discussion of output performance measures is organized around two broad categories, *intermediate outputs* and *final outputs*. Intermediate outputs use *episode*, *material*, and *time* unit-of-service

Table 2.7   An Overview of Performance Measures

Output performance measures	1. Intermediate
	
	  a. Time (unit of service)
	  b. Episode or contact (unit of service)
	  c. Material (unit of service)
	
	2. Final
	
	  a. Service completion

Quality performance measures	1. Outputs with quality dimensions 2. Client satisfaction

Outcome performance measures	1. Intermediate
	
	  a. Numeric counts
	  b. Standardized measures
	  c. Level of functioning (LOF) scales
	  d. Client satisfaction
	
	2. Final
	
	  a. Numeric counts
	  b. Standardized measures
	  c. Level of functioning (LOF) scales

measures. Final outputs use a measure called a *service completion*. The discussion of quality performance measures involves two types of measures, *output measures with quality dimensions* and *client satisfaction*. The discussion of outcome performance measures is organized around two broad categories (*intermediate outcomes* and *final outcomes*) and four distinct types: *numeric counts, standardized measures, level of functioning (LOF) scales,* and *client satisfaction*. These classifications and terms are defined and discussed in detail in subsequent chapters.

Before dealing with the actual development and use of performance measures, however, a discussion of the uses of logic models is necessary. Logic models are a way of linking the selection of performance measures back to assumptions made about the purposes of human service programs and their clients. This discussion is the subject of Chapter 3.

Three

Logic Models, Human Service Programs, and Performance Measurement

Introduction

Although the literature on performance measurement has been around for over two decades now, scholars and practitioners still continue to report difficulties in defining, collecting, aggregating, and using performance measures, particularly outcome performance measures (Bliss, 2007; E. Fisher, 2005; Urban Institute, 2002). From the earliest discussions of performance measurement, it has been clear that conceptualizing and defining outcome performance measures is a difficult task.

The expanded system model (Figure 3.1) was introduced and discussed at length in Chapter 1. In this chapter, the expanded systems model is again utilized to discuss the topic of logic models.

A *logic model* is a visual representation of the sequential stages of a client processing system that makes explicit the interrelationships between the inputs, process, outputs, quality, and outcomes of a human service

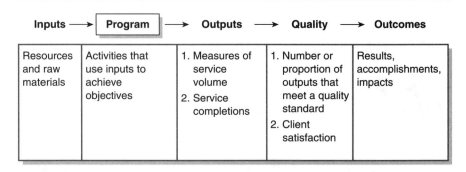

Inputs →	Program →	Outputs →	Quality →	Outcomes
Resources and raw materials	Activities that use inputs to achieve objectives	1. Measures of service volume 2. Service completions	1. Number or proportion of outputs that meet a quality standard 2. Client satisfaction	Results, accomplishments, impacts

Figure 3.1 The Expanded Systems Model

program. In addition, the logic model "provides stakeholders with a road map describing the sequence of related events connecting the need for the planned program with the program's desired results" (University of Wisconsin–Extension, 2003). A logic model is a simple way of connecting a specific human service program to its output, quality, and outcome performance measures.

According to Martin (2008), "logic model" is an umbrella term that includes several different approaches. Figure 3.2 illustrates some of the starting points and ending points for various logic models.

In the *agency strategic plan* approach, the logic model begins with a problem selected by the agency and included in its strategic plan. All subsequent elements of the logic model and the human service program must flow from and support the same set of assumptions as the agency strategic plan. In the *community problem* or *community need* approach, the logic model begins with an identified and clearly defined community problem. All the elements of the logic model must again support the community problem or need. Likewise, in the *social problem* approach,

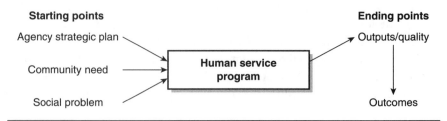

Figure 3.2 Different Types of Logic Models

all elements of the logic model must show how they address the identified social problem. Although there is some overlap between a community problem or need and a social problem, we feel it is important to make the distinction. Community problems or needs tend to be identified, defined, and addressed locally, whereas social problems tend to be national.

The social problem of homelessness can be used to illustrate what is meant by insuring that all components of a logic model are interrelated. In addressing the social problem of homelessness, the inputs (clients) should meet the definition of "homeless" (Without a home address for one day? One week? One month?). The program activities should be designed to ensure that a homeless person is matched with whatever meets the program's definition of a "home" (Shelter? Apartment?). Systematic tracking of outputs should focus on the volume of services provided, on the quality of the services provided, and on the outcomes (results, accomplishments, or impacts) achieved by the human service program (Home finding? Job finding? Medical care?).

Developing a Logic Model

The creation of a logic model for a human service program involves three major tasks:

Task 1: Specify the agency, community, or social problem a human service program is expected to address.

Task 2: Identify the assumptions the program makes about the agency, community, or social problem it addresses.

Task 3: Design the program in a way that makes explicit selected phases of the logic model.

As Figure 3.3 suggests, when these three major tasks are accomplished, the actual development of output, quality, and outcome measures provides accountability information (feedback) on the performance of the

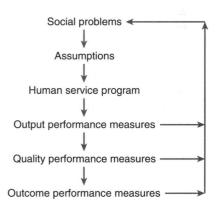

Figure 3.3   The Logic Model Link Between Social Problems, Human Service Programs, and Performance Measures

human service program in addressing the identified agency, community, or social problem.

Task 1: Specify the Agency, Community, or Social Problem

Task 1 involves specifying the agency, community, or social problem a human service program is expected to address. Most human service programs are created to address a specific problem. In defining problems it is useful to distinguish between a condition and a problem. A *condition* is a phenomenon that is present in a community but has not been formally recognized or labeled as a problem. Formal recognition can come from entities such as state legislatures, county boards of supervisors, city councils, school boards, agency boards, and other such formally elected or appointed groups. A *problem,* then, becomes a negatively defined condition (Netting, Kettner, & McMurtry, 2008). The significance of formal recognition is that without it there is usually difficulty building a base of community support or securing funding.

Some social problems are addressed by programs funded with federal, state, or local government dollars through grants and contracts. These include such programs as Head Start (to address the social problem of educational preparation for disadvantaged children), job training (to address the problem of unemployment), and congregate meals for seniors (to address the problem of socially isolated and malnourished elderly people). For human service programs of this type, the language of the law, statute, or ordinance creating the program or its implementing regulations generally specifies the social problem to be addressed. Even when these sources are silent, there may still be expectations from the funding source that a certain social problem is expected to be addressed. In these instances the social problem can still be identified by a reading of federal or state legislative digests or the transcripts of committee hearings and meetings to get a "sense" of funding source expectations and determine whether there is a good fit with the goals and objectives of the agency's programs.

Some federal funding sources are designed to address social problems and social welfare needs from a broader perspective. These federal funding sources are not linked to any particular social problem and are seen more as "funding streams" designed to put resources into a local community to deal with local problems and needs. Examples include the

Social Services Block Grant (SSBG) and the Community Development Block Grant (CDBG). These federal sources fund a variety of programs dealing with a range of social problems. The funding is general and is not tied to any specific social or community problem, yet it is not entirely open ended either and cannot be used just anywhere the local agency feels there is a need.

For federal funding streams of this type, the specified social problem cannot be determined by consulting some law, statute, ordinance, or regulation but must be inferred from the nature of the program funded. For example, if SSBG funding is used to support a child care and protection program, then the social problem the program addresses is child abuse. When SSBG funding is used to support a reduction of elderly neglect, then the social problem the program addresses is that of isolated elderly in the community. When CDBG funds are earmarked for housing, then the problems will have to do with homelessness and people living in substandard housing. Human service programs such as SSBG and CDBG actually wind up addressing many different social problems. As funding from the federal level moves more toward block grants, more human service programs at the state and local levels may find themselves in the position of having to infer the social problems they address rather than finding any explicit statement in federal law or regulation.

Regardless of how the connection is made, it is important for the development of useful performance measures that the link between a specified social problem and the human service program it is expected to address is made explicit.

Task 2: Identify the Program Assumptions

After the connection is made between the specified social problem and the human service program, the second step is to identify the assumptions that are being made about the causes of the problems they address.

Human service programs are also based on assumptions about the *causes* of social problems. Agency, community, and social problems tend to be multifaceted. Problems such as unemployment, poverty, crime, drugs, and others have multiple causes, not just one. On the other hand, human service programs frequently deal with only one cause of a social problem. Unfortunately, the underlying assumptions that human service programs make about the causes of social problems are frequently left unstated. Even when the social problem that a human service program addresses is explicitly stated in law, statute, or ordinance, the assumptions made about the cause of the social problem may go unstated. The challenge for performance measurement—to say nothing of the challenge of developing better human service programs—is that different assumptions about the cause of a problem may call for different programs and different performance measures. For example, the problem of child abuse is often linked to drug and alcohol addiction, to a lack of parenting skills, and to unemployment. Clearly each of these assumptions would lead to a different type of intervention, and each has implications for screening and selection of clients who fit the program's assumptions.

The process of identifying the assumptions that human service programs make about social problems is again likely to be more art than science. Support for assumptions can be drawn from the human service literature on the subject, including theoretical frameworks and models, current research, evaluation studies, and practice experience. The examples that follow are designed to demonstrate how the assumptions that human service programs make about the causes of the social problems they address can affect the selection of performance measures.

Task 3: Design the Program

Task 3 involves designing the program in such a way that the interrelated components of the logic model are made explicit. A program, as defined in Chapter 1, is a major ongoing activity or service with its own sets of policies, goals, objectives, and budgets that produces a defined product or service (Martin, 2008). This definition rules out administrative activities such as personnel, finance, facilities management, clerical pool, and the like from being considered human service programs.

Beyond the guidance provided by this definition, the determination of exactly how many human service programs an organization has is really more art than science and depends on such factors as agency mission, strategic planning goals, budget, personnel, and the like. There is an old "rule of thumb," however, that suggests no organization should have more than 10 programs (Anthony & Young, 1994). The rationale for this cutoff point is that with more than 10 programs, an organization has too many competing priorities (too many goals and objectives) that undermine the chances of any one program being successful.

Identifying and defining human service programs is necessary because performance measurement uses *program* as its unit of analysis. Service efforts and accomplishments (SEA) reporting developed by the Government Accounting Standards Board (GASB) has formally adopted program as the unit of analysis and requires that all performance measures data (both programmatic and financial) be reported by programs. This may mean that when an audit is conducted (depending on the state's use of SEA reporting standards), it's not unlikely that the audit team will be asking not only for balance sheets and financial information, but also for the program's definitions of inputs, activities, outputs, outcomes, and impact and a description of how these indicators are used in program planning and performance measurement.

Other reasons also exist for making programs the unit of analysis for performance measurement. For example, many important stakeholders of human service programs (e.g., elected officials, government funding agencies, and foundations) tend to think of, and to fund, programs. In addition, a canon of the accounting profession, another important stakeholder, is that all government and nonprofit organizations exist for the primary purpose of carrying out programs (Anthony & Young, 2003).

An additional implication of making programs the unit of analysis for performance measurement is that all human service organizations will necessarily have to adopt program budgeting. Program budgeting requires that all costs (both direct and indirect) of operating an organization be allocated to its various programs (Anthony & Young, 2003; Smith & Lynch, 2004). The adoption of program budgeting is necessary to develop the cost per output and cost per outcome ratios suggested by GASB's SEA reporting initiative. An in-depth discussion of program budgeting is beyond the scope of this book, but any basic text on budgeting and financial management for nonprofit organizations (e.g., Anthony & Young, 2003; Smith & Lynch, 2004) should provide an adequate treatment of the subject. And finally, program is the logical unit of analysis in human services because the logic model is designed to lay out the elements of a program in a way that permits performance measurement and program evaluation.

The following three illustrations of logic models are intended to show the relationships between problems, assumptions, human service programs, and the program elements that establish the basis for performance measurement. The first illustration, the increasing use of methamphetamines among high school students, depicts a program that begins with an agency's strategic plan. All elements of the logic model must therefore be consistent with the program as defined in the strategic plan. The second illustration is of a community problem or need. In this community, the Area Agency on Aging has identified deteriorating mental and physical health among the isolated elderly and possible premature placement in nursing care as a priority community problem to be addressed. The third illustration depicts analysis of a social problem, physical violence against children, which is typically addressed by a federal funding source, and is the type of program that would be delivered by either a state or county level department of social services or child protective services.

Agency Strategic Plan Focus

The example in Table 3.1 involves a program designed to address the problem of the increasing use of methamphetamines among high school students. The program is based on the assumption that students are unaware of the consequences of meth use, and is designed to increase awareness and knowledge about its dangers and risks. The problem, assumptions, program, and performance measures are specified. Although funding may be made available from a variety of sources, the problem is clearly stated in the grant or contract award, and the program is expected to address the problem. The program or intervention may not be specified, and a variety of approaches may be possible, each based on the assumptions about the causes of the problem.

Had the assumption been made that teens were experiencing extreme stress and were using meth as a way of reducing stress and feeling good, some modification would be required on output and quality performance measures, while outcome measures may remain the same. The program illustrated provides for education about the risks of meth. An alternative program might focus on teen stress reduction through counseling, peer group discussions, and exercise.

Is one of these assumptions about the cause of the problem of meth use by high school students more correct than the other? Perhaps, perhaps not—ultimately only extensive research and program evaluation will tell. But until there is a clear-cut cause-and-effect relationship established, programs will continue to experiment with various approaches to problem solving, and at this point the only way the effectiveness of alternative approaches can be established is through the type of logic models proposed here.

Table 3.1 Logic Model Beginning With Agency Mission and Strategic Plan

Agency strategic planning goal: Reduction or elimination of steady increases in the use of methamphetamines among high school students over the past 5 years

Assumption: Students are unaware of consequences of meth use

Human service program: Multipronged education and information program aimed at high school students

	Output performance measure	*Quality performance measure*	*Outcome performance measure*
Definitions	Measurements of services provided and completion of all services	Measures of quality of services provided	Demonstrated benefits to those receiving service (results, accomplishments, impacts)
Performance measure	*Media*: Number of radio, TV, and print ads placed *Education*: Number of students attending presentations	Percentage of high school students who rate the program good or excellent	Number or percentage decrease in the number of new meth users among high school students

Community Problem or Need Focus

In the example illustrated in Table 3.2, the Area Agency on Aging (AAA) is making funding available for services to the elderly. The local agency, Independence for Seniors, Inc., already has in place a program called "Elder Outreach," and is attempting to tap into AAA funds to underwrite the costs of delivering these services. If it is determined that this program falls within the range of services that fit with AAA's intent, then the program analysis might look something like that depicted in Table 3.2.

For Independence for Seniors, Inc., in applying for funding it would be their intention to convince AAA personnel that their program works toward the intent and expectations of AAA's plan for providing services to the elderly in the region. Once again, to emphasize the importance of assumptions, the Elder Outreach program assumes that there are at-risk elderly (65 and older) who have unmet needs and are unaware of or unable to access available community services. Another agency in town, Senior Services, Inc., may assume that premature physical and mental deterioration in seniors is caused by social isolation. To prevent further deterioration, they have chosen to provide a congregate meal program with opportunities for games and social interaction before and after meals. Clearly assumptions about premature deterioration have led to two very different forms of intervention. Both may be correct. But the assumptions will lead to different designs for the two programs; different definitions of input, output, quality, and outcome performance measures; and different data sets used to analyze and, hopefully, validate the program. Ultimately that validation will be based on effectiveness of the programs in preventing premature institutionalization among seniors in Jefferson County.

Social Problem Focus

In the third illustration a community-based agency, Child Care, Inc., provides child care and protection services to families at risk of abuse (Table 3.3). One of their programs is a parent training program in which they provide 12 classroom sessions to groups of 10 people or less, covering basic principles of healthy parenting together with professional observation of parents in interaction with their children and follow-up counseling.

In this example the focus of the programs to be funded is driven by goals and objectives established by the funding source—in this case the U.S. Department of Human Services—and passed on to the state Department of

Table 3.2   Logic Model Beginning With Community Need or Problem

Community need or problem: To keep at-risk elderly in Jefferson County in independent living situations for as long as possible

Assumptions: There are at-risk elderly (65 and older) who have unmet needs and are unaware of or unable to access available community services.

Human service program: Elder Outreach, including identifying at-risk elderly, assessment of client need, and transportation

	Output performance measure	*Quality performance measure*	*Outcome performance measure*
Definitions	Measurements of services provided and completion of all services	Measures of quality of services provided	Demonstrated benefits to those receiving service (results, accomplishments, impacts)
Performance measure	*Outreach*: The number of hours of outreach services *Transportation*: The number of trips provided to target group	*Responsiveness*: The number of clients brought into service within 72 hours of initial request The number of clients who arrive at their destinations on time.	Number or percentage of clients who continue in independent living status

Table 3.3   Logic Model Beginning With a Social Problem

Social problem: Violence against children

↓

Program objective: To improve the parenting skills of parents at risk of abusing their children

↓

Assumptions: At-risk parents are deficient in parenting skills, and with improved skills they will no longer physically abuse their children

↓

Human service program: Parental skills training program

↓

	Output performance measure	*Quality performance measure*	*Outcome performance measure*
Definitions	Measurements of services provided and completion of all services	Measures of quality of services provided	Demonstrated benefits to those receiving service (results, accomplishments, impacts)
Performance measure	The number of hours of parental skills training provided	*Reliability:* Parents learn the same content regardless of who teaches the class as measured by post-tests	The number or percentage of at-risk parents who have no further referrals to Child Protective Services for physical abuse to their children

Social Services. Their stated goal is to reduce the incidence of violence against children, and their stated objective is to improve the parenting skills of parents at risk of abusing their children. In exploring this funding opportunity, Child Care, Inc., believes that their parent training program is well positioned to help the Department achieve these goals and objectives. They have defined their output indicators as the number of at-risk parents participating in classroom training and the number observed in live interactions with their children and counseled on parenting techniques. Quality performance will be determined by reliability, meaning that parents learn the same content regardless of who teaches the class as measured by post-tests. The outcome performance measures selected include the number and percentage of at-risk parents who have no further referrals to Child Protective Services for physical abuse to their children.

Another option that might have been considered by planners and program designers at Child Care, Inc., might have been based on the assumption that child abuse is linked to drug and alcohol abuse—that it's not that parents don't know how to parent but that their rational capacities are diminished under the influence of these substances and they tend to react violently when upset. Had that been the direction they had taken, indicators would be structured around overcoming addictions, dealing with stress, and behaving in more rational ways. Since the funding source established the goals and objectives for use of these funds, the burden of proof would be on the program to validate its assumptions by demonstrating that a significant number and percentage of parents who receive these services have no further referrals to Child Protective Services for physical abuse to their children. Also, the state would continue to hold out the expectation that there would be a reduction in the overall incidence of child abuse in the state as recorded by the Child Protective Service division of the state Department of Social Services.

The purpose of this chapter has been to emphasize and reinforce the importance of using the logic model framework to define the elements of a program in a way that will permit program evaluation and performance measurement. In support of this framework we have also attempted to emphasize the importance of a clear understanding of the agency, community, or social problem to be addressed. There are often multiple stakeholders involved in defining the problem, and a clear and explicit statement of assumptions about the causes of the social problem is critical to a sound analysis. In the following chapters we will discuss in more detail the elements of the logic model necessary to performance measurement.

Four

Output Performance Measures

Introduction

With all the emphasis placed on outcomes and outcome performance measures by the federal government, the United Way, and others today, it's easy to overlook the importance of outputs and output performance measures (GPRA, 1993; United Way of America, 2006). The expanded systems model (Figure 4.1) reminds us that output is one of the three dimensions of performance.

Outputs refer to two types of performance measures: (a) the volume of service or product provided, and (b) the number of clients who complete treatment or receive a full complement of services. Much of the literature and online resources on outputs can be found under the heading of "efficiency."

Anyone who has ever operated a small business knows how important output performance measures are. Restaurant operators count the number of meals they serve. Service station operators count the number of gallons of gasoline they pump. Taxi operators count the number of trips their vehicles make. These output performance measures provide feedback to the business operators on how well they are doing in terms of the amount of service provided or the amount of product sold.

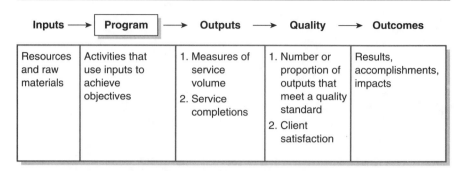

Figure 4.1   The Expanded Systems Model

When outputs and output performance measures are compared with inputs (the costs of doing business), the resulting productivity ratio is a measure of the business's relative efficiency. Outputs and output performance measures serve the same function in human service programs. For example, if output performance is measured by counting the number of counseling sessions provided in one year (say 5,000), and if that number is compared to the cost of providing those counseling sessions (say $200,000), then the cost of each counseling session is $40. This chapter addresses the importance of collecting, using, and reporting these types of data.

What Are Output Performance Measures?

Outputs can be broadly defined as anything that a system (or a human service program) produces (Brody, 2005; Poertner, 2008). As Figure 4.2 illustrates, systems and, by extension, human service programs produce two types of outputs (intermediate and final) and thus require two types of output performance measures. *Intermediate* outputs provide a measure of the products or services provided. *Final* outputs provide a measure of the number of clients who complete treatment or receive a full complement of services. Intermediate outputs and intermediate output performance measures have a *service focus* (What services have been provided?), whereas final outputs and final output performance measures have a *client focus* (What has the client completed?). One can readily recognize the importance of the connection between the two, the intermediate being the prescription of services and the final being the completion, by the client, of the services prescribed.

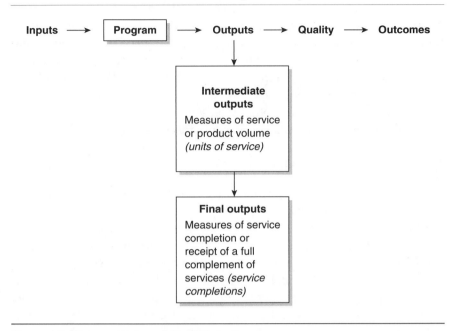

Figure 4.2   Intermediate and Final Outputs

Developing Intermediate Output Performance Measures

Most administrators of human service programs are familiar with units of service. The term *unit of service* has been around at least since the early 1970s. During this period, a study of the use of intermediate output performance measures in state purchase of service contracting was commissioned by the then federal Department of Health, Education, and Welfare. The results were published in a final report titled *The Elusive Unit of Service* (Bowers & Bowers, 1976). The term stuck and joined the human services lexicon as another name for an intermediate output performance measure. So whenever one thinks of a unit of service, one should automatically equate it to an intermediate output, and vice versa.

Definition of Unit of Service

A unit of service is a measure used to determine and report how much service or product is provided by a human service program. In other words, a unit of service is a program-specific measure of service volume. The human services encompass a wide variety of programs. Day care (both child and adult), counseling, parent training, recreation, job training, and others all fall into the category of human services. All need, and can benefit from, measures of service volume, and it is obvious that programs this diverse cannot all use the same unit of service. For this reason, different units of service or intermediate output performance measures have been developed.

Types of Units of Service

Units of service are measured in three different ways: (a) an episode or contact unit, (b) a material unit, and (c) a time unit (Bowers & Bowers, 1976; Brody, 2005; Martin, 2001). Table 4.1 provides examples of these three types of units of service using three common human service programs (information and referral, home-delivered meals, and counseling).

An *episode or contact unit* of service is defined as one contact between a worker and a client. It is used when the recording of client contact information is important but when the actual duration (time) of the contact is not considered important, or when the time and paperwork necessary to collect the data are considered not worth the effort. Most information and referral programs use an episode or contact unit of service.

A *material unit* of service is a tangible resource provided to a client and can include such items as a meal, a food basket, an article of clothing, cash, a prescription, and so forth. Material units are generally considered to be the least precise of the three types of units of service because of the variation that can exist between individual units. For example, the number of items in two food baskets can vary widely, but each basket is still counted as one unit of service.

Table 4.1   Types of Intermediate Outputs (Units of Service)

Service	Type of unit	Example
Information and referral	Episode or contact unit	One contact One referral
Home-delivered meals	Material unit	One meal
Counseling services	Time unit	One hour

A *time unit* can be expressed in minutes, hours, days, weeks, or months, depending on the design and the data needs of individual human service programs. A time unit is generally considered the most precise of the three types of units of service because it is expressed in standardized increments. When time is used as a unit of service, it is important to state whether the time refers only to direct client contact time or if support activity time (e.g., completing paperwork, attending client staffings, etc.) is also included.

Selecting a Unit of Service

Selecting a unit of service for a particular human service program involves several steps. A number of stakeholders are affected by the decision to use a particular unit, so as many as possible should be included in the process. Stakeholders usually include those who work directly with clients, supervisors, managers, administrators, board members, and others who may have occasion to use unit-of-service data. The steps to developing units of service are as follows:

Step 1

Convene a committee that is broadly representative of the stakeholders involved in the particular human service program. Try to ensure that each committee member represents the views of his or her peers and not just his or her own (E. Fisher, 2005).

Step 2

Contact other agencies offering the same services to determine how units have been defined by others and/or consult existing human service taxonomies that have been developed by some states. Brainstorm different units of service, including episode or contact units, material units, and time units. A list of commonly utilized units of service for human service programs is illustrated in Table 4.2.

Step 3

Evaluate each suggested unit of service according to the following five criteria: utility, precision, feasibility, unit cost reporting, and consensus.

Utility. This criterion refers to the extent to which the information generated is considered useful and relevant. Utility has meaning only in relation

Table 4.2   Some Common Units of Service for Human Service Programs

Service	*Unit of service*
Adoption services	One home visit, one adoptive home approved
Advocacy services	One hour of staff time
Assessment services	One assessment
Case management	One hour of staff time
Counseling services	One visit, one contact, one hour
Financial assistance services	One payment
Foster care services	One calendar month
Home health aide services	One visit, one contact, one hour of service
Information and referral services	One contact, one referral
Job training	One class, one session, one hour
Job placement	One unsubsidized job placement
Nursing home services	One day
Shelter care services	One day
Specialized transportation services	One trip, one person transported one-way one time
Weatherization services	One dwelling weatherized

to stakeholders. The most useful unit of service is the one that provides the most relevant information to stakeholders about a human service program. Usefulness is probably the most important criterion of the five listed here.

Precision. As a general rule, the more precise the unit of service, the more precise the information generated about human services programs. The most precise unit is the time unit.

Material and episode units usually result in a loss of precision. The need for precision in units of service must be balanced, however, against the third criterion.

Feasibility. The feasibility criterion refers to the time and effort required by program staff to collect and report unit-of-service data. For example, selecting 15 minutes as the time unit of service (rather than one hour) means that program staff must collect and report four times as much data. In the same vein, if a homeless shelter makes used clothing available to residents, collecting data using a material unit of service (one item of clothing) requires more time and effort than collecting data using a contact unit of service (one resident visiting the clothing center).

Unit cost reporting. Unit costs (how much it costs to provide one unit of service) are used for a variety of purposes in human service programs, including computing break-even points; forecasting revenues, expenses, and caseloads; and purchase-of-service contracting. Ultimately unit cost must be meaningful to planners and budgeters. The relative ability of different units of service to generate needed unit cost data may influence the selection of a particular type (Martin, 2001).

Consensus. Stakeholders of a human service program reach agreement that they will collect, report, use, and respect the unit of service agreed on. A unit of service represents a common language that all operators of a particular human service program agree to speak (E. Fisher, 2005).

Step 4

Test the unit of service selected for a limited period of time with a small number of those who will collect the data to determine the utility, precision, feasibility, unit cost reporting, and consensus around the definitions selected. Table 4.3 illustrates the evaluation criteria and issues to be considered.

Units of Service and Programs of Services

Some human service programs offer multiple services and must use a different unit of service for each program. A good example is adult day care. Adult day care programs can include a transportation component, a congregate meals component, a socialization and recreation component, a health component, and others. A unit of service for adult day care

Table 4.3   Five Criteria for Use in Selecting Units of Service

Criterion	Issues to be addressed
Utility	How will the unit of service be used? What information is needed? How useful is it?
Precision	How precise must the unit be for it to be useful? Can a precise unit be easily determined? How will it be used?
Feasibility	How simple and straightforward will data collection be with the units being considered? Will the time and resources expended be worth the effort? How will it be used?
Unit cost reporting	Can a unit of service be calculated? When a unit cost is calculated, will it be meaningful for planning and budgeting purposes? How will unit costs be used?
Consensus	Is there general agreement among stakeholders about what unit should be selected and how it will be used? Is the unit selected consistent with other providers of a similar service?

might be based on a time unit—1 day, for example. On the basis of this time unit of service, if each of 20 seniors participates in the program five times during a week, the adult day care program would generate 100 units of service, or intermediate outputs, for the week. But this unit of service (1 day) does not actually say much about what the adult day care program really does.

Table 4.4 illustrates how a unit of service, or intermediate output performance measure, report might appear for an adult day care program when the various service components are separately identified and reported.

As Table 4.4 demonstrates, a more comprehensive, meaningful, and powerful picture emerges. Now units of service, or intermediate output performance measures, are used not just for accountability purposes but also as a communications device. An additional benefit of using units of service in this manner is that the adult day care center administrator now has considerably more data about the program that can be used for planning and budgeting purposes.

Table 4.4   A Monthly Report on Adult Day Care Services

Transportation	14	260 trips	18.6 trips per client
Meals	20	352 meals	17.6 meals per client
Socialization and recreation	16	1,289 hours	80.6 hours per client
Health screenings	6	19 screenings	3.2 screenings per client

Final Output Performance Measures

Final outputs are probably easiest to understand when compared to a university. A university can seem to be relatively productive when measured by the number of students who register for classes, but it doesn't mean a lot if, say, more than half of them drop out before the end of the semester. In this case, the university would be providing a high volume of units of service (hours of instruction), but would be considered to be unproductive in terms of completion of courses. In the same way, a human service program can provide a high volume of service as measured by units of service, but be relatively unproductive if few clients complete the treatment process. When dropout rates are high, the results tend to be minimal and are generally costly. Human service organizations need to keep track of their "customers" by tracking those that enter the system and those that complete the services prescribed. Later we will discuss the measurement of improvement as well.

Defining a Service Completion

A service completion, or a final output performance measure, can be defined as *one client completing treatment or receiving a full complement of services* (Ables & Murphy, 1981; Kettner et al., 2008; Kettner & Martin, 1993). Frequently human service programs do not define a service completion; this presents a problem for performance measurement. The concept of a service completion has been used in the field of medicine for a long time. In the practice of medicine, a physician may prescribe a particular medication that a patient is supposed to take for 30 days because this length of time is considered necessary for the treatment to effect a cure. Consequently, if the patient stops taking the medication after

10 days, no expectation should exist that the treatment will be effective. The concept of "against medical advice" is generally understood and accepted. By analogy, if a client of a human service program does not complete treatment or does not receive a full complement of services, no expectation should exist that the treatment will be effective. Take the case of a parenting skills training program for abusive and neglecting parents. If the training program consists of 10 sessions, and if all 10 sessions are considered essential to altering abusive and neglecting behavior, then it is important to know whether each client completed the full 10 sessions. But for service completions to be measured, they must first be defined.

Developing Service Completions

Although some services (such as training) typically define a service completion, many services do not. As Table 4.5 illustrates, there are two approaches to determining a service completion: (a) the standardized approach and (b) the case plan approach. The selection of the appropriate approach depends on whether the treatment or service is standardized or variable.

Table 4.5 Two Approaches to Developing Service Completions

Approach	When used	Definition of a service completion	Example
Standardized approach	When a minimum number of units (time, episode, or material) are required for clients to complete treatment	One client completing treatment or receiving a full complement of services required for the program	One client completing 12 weeks of training in basic computer skills
Case plan approach	When clients receive varied units of service depending on individualized needs	One client completing all the services prescribed in the case plan	A couple contemplating divorce agrees to work with a counselor until a final decision is made

In the standardized approach, a client must receive a minimum amount of prescribed service to complete treatment. Only at this point can a service completion report or a description of a final output be recorded. Past experience with intermediate outputs (units of service) may be of some help in determining the minimum amount of prescribed service required to complete treatment or to receive a full complement of services. Training, child care, and some types of counseling are good examples of the standardized approach.

For example, in human service programs that use a time unit of service (e.g., hour, day, week, and month) or an episode unit, a certain number of units is required for a client to complete the program or to receive a full complement of services. In each case it will depend on the type of problem and service, and the objectives of the program. A preschool program designed to teach 10 specific skills may require, perhaps, 20 to 25 sessions. A program designed to teach young families how to communicate may require a minimum of 12 sessions.

The second approach to developing final output performance measures or service completions is the case plan approach. Many human service programs do not have a standardized, or minimum, amount of service that clients must receive to complete treatment. For example, in a counseling program, some families may need many months of counseling sessions and support services to resolve their problems, complete treatment, and receive a full complement of services. Others with less severe problems may require significantly fewer sessions, perhaps only a few weeks. Likewise, adolescents who are severely disturbed may need years of residential treatment; others may need only a short stay away from their homes. In situations such as these, it may be more useful to think of a service completion as one client completing an individual case plan. When a client has completed a case plan, a full complement of services has been provided and a service completion is recorded for the client. Clearly the case management approach to determining final outputs does not provide the neat, comparable unit that the standardized approach does, and accommodations have to be made when determining unit costs for these services. In all cases defining final outputs should follow the same step-by-step guides as provided for defining intermediate units of service.

The case plan approach can also be applied to human service programs such as case management for persons who are in nursing care or are receiving other long-term treatment. In these settings an expectation typically exists that clients will remain in treatment for extended (perhaps indefinite) periods. Rather than look at long-term case management services as prescribing years of treatment, services can be divided into discrete episodes lasting, for example, for 3 months. After 3 months of case management services, a client is said to have received a full complement of services (or dropped out) and a service completion or dropout is recorded for the client.

Service Completions and Client Outcomes

Service completions are important not only in measuring outputs, but they also play a role in the measurement of outcomes. We will discuss outcome performance measurement in more detail in subsequent chapters, but as a general rule outcome performance measures should be assessed only on those clients who *complete treatment or receive a full complement of services.* This position is in keeping with the medical analogy discussed earlier in the chapter. No expectation should exist that a human service program will be effective with clients who do not complete treatment or receive a full complement of services.

The use of service completions in determining which clients should be involved in outcome performance measurement is in keeping with Rossi, Lipsey, and Freeman's (2004) notion of a comprehensive evaluation. Rossi et al. make the point that one cannot draw valid conclusions about the effectiveness of a human service program if the program is not implemented as designed. Service completions distinguish between those clients who experience a human service program as it was designed and those who do not.

Although it is important to capture evaluation data on "service non-completers," the data collected should be used differently from that collected from "completers." Data on service non-completers may provide useful insights into the operation of human service programs and may lead to important discoveries and program improvements. Such discoveries and improvements, however, do not affect those clients who have already completed treatment or dropped out.

In the following chapter, the subjects of quality and quality performance measures are discussed. As the chapter makes clear, the quality of human service programs is a major factor in determining ways in which outputs and outcomes are achieved.

Five

Quality Performance Measures

Introduction

Consider the following situation involving two eligibility workers employed in the same human service program. The first worker assesses an average of four clients per hour; the second worker assesses three clients per hour. Which worker is more productive? The efficiency perspective of accountability suggests that the first worker is. But what if the first worker makes twice as many errors as the second worker? Errors require additional staff time and resources to correct; errors can result in lost revenue due to client ineligibility. Now, which worker is more productive? Historically, the quality perspective of accountability has held that the second worker is more productive (Crosby, 1985; Deming, 1986; Juran, 1989).

Quality performance measures are designed to keep administrators of human service programs from falling into what the quality management proponents call the "efficiency trap." Focusing only on the efficiency perspective of performance accountability, these advocates argue, inevitably leads to declining service quality. Declining service quality, in turn, leads to less reliable services. Less reliable services leads to less timely services, more errors, more rework, increased client complaints, more time and money spent on resolving client complaints, and, in the end, lower overall productivity.

What Is Quality?

The concept of quality is composed of a number of somewhat elusive dimensions. When people disagree about the quality of something, be it a new car or a human service program, the disagreement is frequently because they hold different views about what constitutes quality. To a great extent, quality—like beauty—lies in the eye of the beholder. Because of the relative nature of quality, a final arbiter of what constitutes quality is needed. In quality management, customers are usually regarded as the final arbiters (Martin, 1993a, 1993b).

Quality management, because it was developed by business, assumes that the customer and the payer are the same. Human service programs are somewhat unique in that they have two classes of customers: *clients* and *funding sources.* The reasons for this duality is that client customers receive services, but frequently do not pay for them, whereas funding source customers pay for services, but generally do not receive them. For the purposes in this chapter, the focus will be on client customers in order to remain as faithful to the basic concepts of quality management as possible.

Because the concept is multidimensional, two initial hurdles must be overcome before quality performance measures can be developed for human service programs. The two hurdles are (a) identifying the various dimensions of quality and (b) determining which ones are most important.

The Dimensions of Quality

At least 15 generally recognized quality dimensions can be identified (Table 5.1). Some of these dimensions relate to quality issues in products and services generally; others apply more specifically to human service programs (Martin, 1993a). For example, *tangibles,* or the appearance of facilities, equipment, personnel, and so on, is generally considered to be an important quality dimension to customers, whether public, private, or non-profit. On the other hand, *humaneness* and *empathy,* quality dimensions that have to do with the protection of a client's sense of self-worth or feelings, may well be more important in human service programs than in other service areas.

Accessibility is another quality dimension frequently dealt with in the human services, and which is often the reason for opening branch offices. What good is a human service program, people ask, if it is not reasonably accessible to those people who need it?

Table 5.1   Some Dimensions of Quality

Dimension	Definition	Example
Accessibility	The program is easy to access or acquire.	A branch office is not more than 10 minutes away.
Assurance	Program staff are friendly, polite, considerate, and knowledgeable.	Receptionist knows clients' names.
Communication	Program information is provided in simple, understandable language.	Printed materials are screened for elimination of jargon, etc.
Competency	Program staff possess the requisite knowledge and skills.	All counselors have at least a master's degree in their field.
Conformity	The service meets established standards.	Meals provided meet appropriate Recommended Daily Allowances.
Courtesy	Program staff demonstrate respect toward clients.	Client first names are not used without permission.
Deficiency	The program is missing a characteristic or element.	Transportation is not provided to the center.
Durability	The program's performance or results do not dissipate quickly.	Couples receiving counseling are still together one year later.
Empathy	Program staff attempt to understand clients' needs and provide individualized attention.	Counselors demonstrate knowledge of client needs from one appointment to the next.
Humaneness	The program is provided in a manner that protects clients' dignity and sense of self-worth.	Staff never act in a condescending manner toward clients.

(Continued)

Table 5.1 (Continued)

Dimension	Definition	Example
Performance	The program accomplishes its intended purposes.	Clients are able to overcome their addictions.
Reliability	The program operates in a dependable and reliable manner.	Classes offered always have the same trainer and curriculum.
Responsiveness	The program delivery is timely.	Clients do not have to wait an unreasonable time to receive services.
Security	The program is provided in a safe setting free from risk or danger.	Facilities are located in safe neighborhoods.
Tangibles	The appearance of the facilities, equipment, personnel, and published materials involved in program delivery is appropriate.	The reception room is pleasant and inviting. Printed materials are attractive.

With all these competing quality dimensions, how do you determine which ones are most important? The best answer to this question is to ask your customers (clients). However, some research suggests that in general, two quality dimensions appear to be important to the customers of most human service programs: *reliability* (consistency) and *responsiveness* (timeliness).

As a quality dimension, reliability refers to how consistently the expectations of clients are satisfied. One of the reasons that McDonald's restaurants are so popular worldwide is because of their reliability; consumers get the same quality products at all their outlets. Reliability works the same way in the human service. If clients in a human service program view empathy as an important quality dimension, they will also expect reliability (consistency) in the level of empathy demonstrated by program staff from one contact to the next. What then does reliability mean for human service programs? Reliability essentially means providing services in a consistent fashion; always being friendly, polite, and considerate (assurance); always attempting to understand client needs (empathy); always speaking with clients in understandable language (communication); and so forth. The emphasis here is *always,* not just occasionally or when staff happen to be in the mood.

When human service programs are operated in a reliable manner, clients whose quality judgments are formed on the basis of this dimension will tend to rate the service quality as high. When human service programs are unreliable (too much variation), clients whose quality judgments are formed on the basis of this dimension will tend to rate the service quality as low.

Responsiveness means being timely. Being responsive entails providing services with a minimum of waiting time. *Waiting,* referred to in quality management as "cycle time," is the total elapsed time between when a client needs or wants a service and when the service is actually received. Waiting, or cycle time, means not just physically waiting in some line but waiting in any and all forms (Table 5.2). When a human service is provided in a responsive or timely fashion, clients whose quality judgments are formed on the basis of this dimension will tend to rate the service quality as high.

Types of Quality Performance Measures

Two basic approaches exist to developing quality performance measures: (a) the *outputs with quality dimensions* approach and (b) the *client satisfaction* approach (Table 5.3). The outputs with quality dimensions approach utilizes data from agency records; the client satisfaction approach utilizes data from client satisfaction surveys.

Table 5.2   Examples of Waiting or Cycle Time Issues

- Waiting for a food stamp application to be processed
- Waiting for a Supplemental Security Insurance (SSI) check to arrive
- Waiting for a preschool voucher to be issued
- Waiting for a case manager to call back
- Waiting on the telephone to speak to a "real" person

Table 5.3   Two Types of Quality Performance Measures

---

1. *Outputs with quality dimensions*
   - Data source: agency records
2. *Client satisfaction*
   - Data source: client satisfaction surveys

Outputs With Quality Dimensions Approach

The outputs with quality dimensions approach involves extending intermediate output performance measures (units of service) to include quality dimensions. This process sounds a lot more complicated than it really is. A simple three-step process is all that is required. These steps are summarized in Table 5.4.

Some examples will help in demonstrating and explicating each of these steps. For the sake of continuity (reliability), the three human service programs—information and referral, home-delivered meals, and counseling—used as examples of intermediate output performance measures in Chapter 4 are again used here.

Step 1: Select Quality Dimensions

Most human service programs will probably want—at a minimum— to select the quality dimensions of reliability and responsiveness or timeliness. The selection of other quality dimensions (e.g., assurance, competency, empathy, tangibles, etc.) will depend largely on the type of human service program and the preferences of customers.

Table 5.4   Steps in Creating Outputs With Quality Dimensions

---

Step 1: Select the quality dimensions to be used.
Step 2: Translate the quality dimensions to the specific characteristics of the human service program.
Step 3: Graft the quality dimensions to intermediate output performance measures.

Step 2: Translate Quality Dimensions

Each quality dimension selected must be translated into some characteristic of the human service program that is important to customers. For example, what does reliability and responsiveness mean for an information and referral program, a home-delivered meals program, or a counseling program?

1. *Information and referral*
   a. Reliability might mean that the referrals made are appropriate (no referrals to agencies at which the caller is ineligible for service) or that referrals result in clients actually receiving services.
   b. Responsiveness might mean that callers connect on the first attempt (no busy signals).

2. *Home-delivered meals*
   a. Reliability might mean that meals are delivered hot (at some minimum temperature).
   b. Responsiveness might mean that meals are delivered on time (within 10 minutes of scheduled delivery time).

3. *Counseling*
   a. Reliability might mean that clients see the same counselor each time.
   b. Responsiveness or timeliness might mean that clients are not kept waiting (more than 10 minutes) for scheduled appointments.

The parenthetical comments included for each of these quality dimensions serve two purposes. First, they assist in further defining and specifying the quality dimensions. Second, they also assist stakeholders in interpreting the resulting quality performance measures. Parenthetical comments such as these can be made part of the actual quality dimension itself.

Step 3: Graft Quality Dimensions

The translated quality dimensions are grafted, or attached, to the existing intermediate output performance measures (episode, material, or time units of service) designated for the particular human service program. In Chapter 4, the units of service designated for the three human service programs were

- Information and referral: one contact or one referral
- Home-delivered meals: one meal
- Counseling: one hour

Table 5.5 illustrates how quality dimensions might be grafted to each of these units of service.

Human service programs that use time as the unit of service or intermediate output performance measure represent something of a challenge. Experience has shown that some creativity and stretching may be necessary to make the process work. The best rule of thumb is to be guided by common sense. A quality performance measure that appears contrived may not command much respect from stakeholders and probably should be avoided. If a simple logical fit cannot be made between a quality dimension and a particular unit of service (e.g., time), consideration should be given to either (a) selecting another unit of service or (b) adopting the client satisfaction approach.

Client Satisfaction Approach

If the outputs with quality dimensions approach prove cumbersome, produce contrived results, or simply will not work, the client satisfaction

Table 5.5   Grafting Quality Dimensions to Intermediate Output Measures (units of service)

1. **Information and Referral**	
a. Reliability	One appropriate referral, or one referral resulting in service
b. Responsiveness	One caller connecting the first time
2. **Home-delivered meals**	
a. Reliability	One meal delivered hot
b. Responsiveness	One meal delivered on time
3. **Counseling**	
a. Reliability	One hour of service with the counselor of record
b. Responsiveness	One hour of service when appointment started on time

approach can be used as an alternative. The client satisfaction approach also involves a simple three-step process with the first two steps being the same as for the outputs with quality dimensions approach. The third step diverges in that it requires the construction and administration of a client satisfaction survey. Again, the best way to explain this three-step process is by resorting to examples. The same three human service programs (information and referral, home-delivered meals, and counseling) are again used.

Step 1: Select Quality Dimensions

The first step is to identify the important quality dimensions. Let us assume that client stakeholders of all three human service programs identify reliability and responsiveness or timeliness as important quality dimensions.

Step 2: Translate Quality Dimensions

Each of the two selected quality dimensions (reliability and responsiveness or timeliness) is translated into significant characteristics of each of the three human service programs. Let's assume that client stakeholders also identify the same characteristics as were used in the outputs with quality dimensions approach:

1. *Information and referral*
   a. Reliability: Referrals made are appropriate.
   b. Responsiveness: Callers connect on the first attempt.

2. *Home-delivered meals*
   a. Reliability: Meals arrive hot.
   b. Responsiveness: Meals arrive on time.

3. *Counseling*
   a. Reliability: Clients see the same counselor.
   b. Responsiveness: Clients are not kept waiting.

Step 3: Develop Survey Questions

A survey questionnaire is then developed that includes one overall general satisfaction question and at least one specific question for each quality dimension (Table 5.6). The purpose of the overall general satisfaction question is to allow statistics to be used to determine which quality dimensions are most important to clients. An agency with multiple human service programs would simply replicate the process for each program.

Table 5.6 Client Satisfaction Survey Questionnaire

Information and Referral Program

1. Overall, how satisfied are you with the information and referral program?

   Very dissatisfied   Very satisfied

   1   2   3   4   5

2. Do your contacts with the information and referral program result in referrals to agencies whose services you are eligible for?

   Almost never   Almost always

   1   2   3   4   5

3. When you call the information and referral program, do you usually get connected on the first attempt?

   Almost never   Almost always

   1   2   3   4   5

Home-Delivered Meals Program

1. Overall, how satisfied are you with the home-delivered meals program?

   Very dissatisfied   Very satisfied

   1   2   3   4   5

2. Do your home-delivered meals arrive hot?

   Almost never   Almost always

   1   2   3   4   5

3. Do your home-delivered meals arrive on time (within 10 minutes of scheduled delivery times)?

   Almost never   Almost always

   1   2   3   4   5

Counseling Program

1. Overall, how satisfied are you with the counseling program?

   Very dissatisfied   Very satisfied

   1   2   3   4   5

2. Do you see the same counselor each time you visit the agency?

   Almost never   Almost always

   1   2   3   4   5

3. Do your counseling sessions start on time (within 10 minutes of the scheduled time)?

   Almost never   Almost always

   1   2   3   4   5

In the client satisfaction approach, questions and responses must be carefully phrased. The questions and response categories shown in Table 5.6 are meant to be only examples of one approach—not the only approach or even the best approach. In addition, unless all clients are surveyed, care must be taken to ensure that a representative sample is drawn. Any basic text on survey research should provide the necessary guidance concerning question phrasing, response category development, and sampling.

In summary, the issues of quality, quality performance accountability, and quality performance measurement are important issues that are easy to overlook when there is too much emphasis on efficiency. Human service agencies and programs have demonstrated that they can become more efficient if the right incentives are present, but it is often at the expense of quality. To restate a principle from earlier chapters, in applying the principles of performance accountability and performance measurement, it is important to send the message that all three dimensions (efficiency, quality, effectiveness) are equally important.

Six

Outcome Performance Measures

Introduction

It is absolutely critical that anyone working with performance measurement understand the concept of outcome. Outcome is a measure of effectiveness. It describes whether or not the services provided did any good. For many years government and private funders continued to give money to both government and nonprofit human service programs simply on the assumption that they had good intentions and were probably doing no harm. Eventually, however, questions began to emerge about whether the billions being spent for human service programs nationally were resulting in people being better off after receiving services than they were before. When it was discovered that programs couldn't demonstrate that clients were better off for having received services, the federal, state, and local actions described in Chapter 2 began to take hold. Today, stakeholders from funders and board members to direct service personnel place primary importance on effectiveness and achievement of outcomes in human service programs.

What Are Outcome Performance Measures?

Referring back to Chapter 2, outcome performance measures have been broadly defined for the purposes of service efforts and accomplishments (SEA) reporting as the results, accomplishments, or impacts that are attributable, at least partially, to a service or program (GASB, 2008). For purposes of human service programs, however, a more specific client focus is generally adopted. Attempts to link the outcomes of human service programs with a client focus have historically gone by such names as *client outcomes* and *client outcome monitoring*. These approaches have included assessments of client impacts and quality-of-life changes in clients as the intended outcomes of human service programs (e.g., Carter, 1983; Else, Groze, Hornby, Mirr, & Wheetlock, 1992; Kettner, Moroney, & Martin, 2008; A. Millar, Hatry, & Koss, 1977a, 1977b; R. Millar & Millar, 1981; Poertner, 2008; Schainblatt, 1977; Tatara, 1980). By blending these various themes together, we can derive the following operational definition of outcome performance measures: *the results, accomplishments, or impacts of human service programs as measured by quality-of-life changes in clients.*

Client Problems Versus Client End States

In the human services, clients are generally seen as having problems. For example, a client may be said to have an addiction problem, a housing problem, an income problem, a child care problem, or some other problem or combination of problems. This problem approach is well suited to diagnosis and treatment, but is less useful in thinking about the results, accomplishments, or impacts of human service programs. Reporting to board members, for example, that 150 clients were helped with their problems may be accurate information, but it is not as useful as informing them that 150 clients had achieved a certain precise and defined outcome (quality-of- life change).

Quality-of-life changes can be thought of as either movement toward some desirable client condition, status, behavior, functioning, attitude, feeling, or perception or movement away from some undesirable client condition, status, behavior, functioning, attitude, feeling, or perception. This client end state or outcome approach has the advantages of emphasizing the results, accomplishments, or impacts of human service programs as well as forcing consideration about what will actually be measured (i.e., client conditions, status, behaviors, functioning, attitudes, feelings, or perceptions).

Table 6.1 provides some examples of client quality-of-life changes that might serve as outcome performance measures. Table 6.1 also demonstrates how desirable and undesirable client conditions, status,

Table 6.1   Examples of Quality-of-Life Changes in Clients

Client quality-of-life changes	Definition	Examples of movement toward some positive change	Examples of movement away from some undesirable change
Condition	External or internal circumstance or factor	A homeless client moving into a homeless shelter or apartment	A decrease in the number of nights a homeless person spends on the streets
Status	Position, rank, or standing	An unemployed client getting a job	A decrease in the number of days of work missed by an employed substance-abusing client
Behavior	A person's actions	An improvement in grade point average for a juvenile client	A decrease in the number of days a juvenile client misses school
Functioning	The way in which a person fulfills a role	An increase in the number of incidents where a client uses rational problem-solving skills	A decrease in the number of times a client argues with spouse
Attitude	A person's disposition, opinion, or mental set	An increase in a juvenile client's acceptance of the value of education	A decrease in the number of times a juvenile client makes positive references to a gang
Feeling	Awareness, consciousness, or sensation	An increase in the number of times a client expresses feelings of belonging	A decrease in the number of times a client expresses feeling of powerlessness over his or her environment
Perception	Ideas or concepts achieved through the senses	An increase in the number of times a client expresses feelings of self-esteem	A decrease in the number of times a client expresses negative perceptions about him- or herself

behaviors, functioning, attitudes, feelings, and perceptions are really two sides of the same coin, and may be capable of serving as outcome performance measures.

The Four Types of Outcome Performance Measures

Outcome performance measures can be divided into four major types. As shown in Table 6.2, these are numeric counts, standardized measures, level of functioning (LOF) scales, and client satisfaction (Kettner & Martin, 1993; Kuechler, Velasquez, & White, 1988).

Numeric counts are simple nominal counts of the numbers of clients who achieve a quality-of-life change. Standardized measures are normed before-and-after tests used to measure quality-of-life changes in clients. Level of functioning (LOF) scales are before-and-after tests (frequently unnormed) created by an agency or program to measure quality-of-life changes in clients. When it is used as an outcome performance measure, client satisfaction refers to client self-reporting about quality-of-life changes.

Different types of outcome performance measures are more or less amenable to measuring different types of client quality-of-life changes, as illustrated in Table 6.2. For example, numeric counts are generally

Table 6.2   Uses of Outcome Performance Measures

Type of outcome performance measure	Purpose
Numeric count	Generally used to measure client conditions, statuses, or behaviors
Standardized measure	Generally used to measure client feelings, attitudes, and perceptions
Level of functioning (LOF) scale	Generally used to measure client or family functioning
Client satisfaction	Generally used to measure client perceptions

used to count up the number of clients who meet the definitions of conditions, statuses, or behaviors as illustrated in Table 6.1. Standardized measures that have been formally researched and are able to establish norms are generally used to measure some of the softer findings concerning client feelings, attitudes, and perceptions. LOF scales are generally used to measure client or family functioning where it is possible to determine the way in which a person or members of a family fulfill their roles. LOF scales are also used when standardized measures are not available or when they are not suitable for use with particular target populations because of age, ethnicity, or other factors. Finally, client satisfaction is generally used when measuring client perceptions about quality-of-life changes. These findings are generally considered to be the least reliable because the frame of reference for responses can change from client to client. It is worth reiterating here that outcome performance measures should be compiled and reported only on service completions (i.e., clients who complete treatment or who receive a full complement of services).

Intermediate and Final Outcome Performance Measures

The four types of outcome performance measures can also be divided into two broad categories depending on their use as either (a) intermediate outcome performance measures or (b) final outcome performance measures. This is illustrated in Table 6.3.

Intermediate outcome performance measures assess quality-of-life changes in clients immediately upon completion of treatment or receipt of a full complement of services. In other words, intermediate outcome performance measures provide an assessment of treatment effects (United Way of America, 2006). Take, for example, the case of a child in residential care. An intermediate outcome performance measure attempts to assess quality-of-life changes (conditions or behaviors) in the child immediately on leaving the program or after receiving a full complement of services. Perhaps the child is able to demonstrate a great deal more self-control at the point of discharge than at the point of admission.

However, not all treatment effects are readily discernable immediately upon completion of treatment or the receipt of a full complement of

Table 6.3   Uses of Performance Measures for Intermediate or Final Outcomes

Type of performance measure	Use
Numeric counts	Intermediate and final outcome performance measures
Standardized measures	Intermediate and final outcome performance measures
Level of functioning (LOF) scale	Intermediate and final outcome performance measures
Client satisfaction	Intermediate performance measures only

services (Benveniste, 1994). Also, some funding sources and stakeholders are interested in long-term effects (University of Wisconsin–Extension, 2003). What is the child's behavior like 6 months or 1 year following completion of the program? In order to determine these long-term effects, there is a need to capture data about outcomes at some follow-up point (e.g., 3 months, 6 months, 1 year, etc.). Some human service programs may use the same measure as both an intermediate outcome and a final outcome; other human service programs may have different measures.

In theory, all four types of outcome performance measures can be used to capture data on either intermediate or final outcomes. In actual practice, however, client satisfaction is rarely used as a final outcome performance measure (Kettner & Martin, 1993; Kuechler et al., 1988; Nurius & Hudson, 1993). This finding may reflect a belief of human service administrators that client satisfaction data are more meaningful at the point of completion of service than they are in a follow-up assessment.

Selecting Outcome Performance Measures

A three-step process is suggested for the development of outcome performance measures:

Step 1: Convene Stakeholder Focus Group

A focus group broadly representative of the stakeholders of the human service program should be convened. Prior to meeting, the focus group's members should become familiar with the most recent and widely accepted research dealing with conceptual frameworks, theories, evaluations, and practice experience pertaining to the problem and the human service program.

Step 2: Assess Outcome Performance Measures

Potential outcome performance measures should be identified, listed, discussed, and considered by the group. As part of this process, the social problem the human service program addresses and the assumptions made about the social problem should be made explicit. The same five criteria used in assessing units of service should be used in assessing the value of outcome indicators: utility, precision, feasibility, unit cost reporting, and consensus.

Step 3: Select Outcome Performance Measures

The group should eliminate those outcome performance measures that are clearly not acceptable because they do not represent appropriate outcomes for the program or because they are too difficult or costly to retrieve. The group should arrive at a consensus on the one or two "best" outcome performance measures for the human service program.

Cause-and-Effect Relationships

The use and reporting of outcome performance measures for human service programs implies a cause-and-effect relationship. A human service program is the cause, and the implied effect is a quality-of-life change in clients. This implied cause-and-effect relationship poses some potential risks for human service programs.

In discussing the implied cause-and-effect relationship between human service programs and outcome performance measures, the GASB (2008) offers a word of caution: "For many outcomes, a definite cause-and-effect relationship . . . cannot be established because of their complex nature and factors beyond the control of the entity [program] that affect the outcome being measured" (p. 22). GASB is saying that although an individual human service program may produce and report outcome performance measures, the program itself may not be the sole cause of the outcome. Consider the following scenario.

The outcome performance measure for a job training program is placement in full-time, unsubsidized employment. Twenty-five trainees in a job training program are hired into full-time, unsubsidized employment immediately on graduating from the program. Twenty-five job placements are recorded and reported for the program. The same week the 25 trainees graduate, a major new manufacturing plant opens nearby and begins recruiting to fill 1,000 permanent full-time jobs. All 25 graduating trainees wind up hired by the new plant. Is the job training program the cause of the 25 trainees being employed? Or is the new manufacturing plant (a factor totally unrelated to the job training program) the cause of the 25 trainees being employed?

One could probably argue that both the job training program and the new plant are causes of the 25 trainees being employed. If the job training program had not adequately prepared the 25 trainees, they might not have been hired. Likewise, if the new manufacturing plant had not opened, the 25 trainees might not have been hired, irrespective of how adequately the job training program had prepared them.

The point of this illustration is that the use of outcome performance measures by human service programs does not imply a one-to-one cause-and-effect relationship between the program and the outcome. The job training program should properly take credit for the job placements, but it should also work to ensure that its stakeholders understand that the program may not be the only cause. One might argue that human service programs should simply "take the credit" whenever possible and not bother with making disclaimers. The problem with this approach is illustrated by reversing the job training scenario. Suppose, for example, that the 25 trainees had graduated at the height of an economic recession, that the manufacturing plant never opened, and that only 5 (20%) of the graduating trainees found employment. Should the stakeholders of the job training program conclude that the program is ineffective? No, of course not! Factors other than the program, in this case a bad economy, affected the program's outcome performance measures—job placements. If human service programs do not want to shoulder 100% of the blame for the lack of program effectiveness due to factors beyond their control, it is probably wise not to take 100% of the credit.

Educating stakeholders about what outcome performance measures really are, and what they are not, is an important—and little discussed—problem associated with their use by human service programs. In a classic report describing initial findings from pilot outcome performance measurement projects conducted by federal departments under the Government Performance and Results Act (1993), the National Academy of Public Administration (Hatry & Wholey, 1994) commented that

> outcome indicators will, in general, not tell the extent to which the program has actually caused the observed outcomes. . . . We suspect that the lack of understanding as to what the outcome indicators tell, and what they do not tell, will continue to cause confusion at all levels of the federal government and outside (e.g., with the media)—leading to excessive expectations as to what regular performance measurement can do. (p. 4)

Social Indicators as Final Outcome Performance Measures

Some states and communities have experimented with using social indicators as final outcome performance measures for human service programs. *Social indicators* can be defined generally as data that enable evaluative judgments to be made about social problems in a community or state (Miller, 1991). Social indicator data typically draw from the U.S. Census, *The County and City Data Book, Sourcebook of Criminal Justice Statistics,* and many other resources from all fields. Most of these resources are available online. Armed with social indicator data, citizens, advocacy groups, elected officials, and other stakeholders can make evaluative judgments about whether social problems in a community or state are getting better, getting worse, or staying about the same. Provided the same types of data are collected, comparisons can also be made between communities or states.

One of the more recent attempts to develop and use social indicator data has been developed by the Steering Committee for the Review of Government Services Provision (SCRGSP) of the Commonwealth of Australia (SCRGSP, 2007). The Committee has developed a number of strategic areas for action, beginning at the prenatal stage and going through adult economic participation and development. Australia is attempting to track each of these indicators, which were chosen for their potential to have a significant impact on Indigenous disadvantage. The strategic areas are identified in Table 6.4.

Table 6.4   Social Indicators Used by the Commonwealth of Australia

Strategic areas for action	Strategic change indicators
Early child development and growth (prenatal to age 3)	Injury and preventable disease Infant mortality Birth weight Hearing impediments Children with tooth decay
Early school engagement and performance (preschool to Grade 3)	Preschool and early learning School attendance Grade 3 literacy and numeracy
Positive childhood and transition to adulthood	Grades 5 and 7 literacy and numeracy Retention at Grade 9 Indigenous cultural studies in school curriculum and involvement of Indigenous people in development and delivery of Indigenous studies Juvenile diversions as a proportion of all juvenile offenders Transition from school to work
Substance use and misuse	Alcohol consumption and harm Tobacco consumption and harm Drug and other substance use and harm
Functional and resilient families and communities	Children on care and protection orders Repeat offending Access to primary health care Mental health Proportion of Indigenous people with access to their traditional lands Participation in organized sport, arts, or community group activities Engagement with service delivery

Strategic areas for action	Strategic change indicators
Effective environmental health systems	Rates of diseases associated with poor environmental health (including water- and food-borne diseases, trachoma, tuberculosis, and rheumatic heart disease)
	Access to clean water and functional sewerage
	Overcrowding in housing
Economic participation and development	Employment (full-time/part-time) by sector (public/private), industry, and occupation
	Self-employment and Indigenous business
	Indigenous-owned or -controlled land
	Governance capacity and skills
	Case studies in governance arrangements

Although initiatives such as Australia's strategic areas for action are certainly innovative and should be applauded, they also come with risks. The risk is, of course, the implied cause-and-effect relationships between human service programs and the social indicators that are used as final outcome performance measures. An individual human service program is probably not going to have much effect on a social indicator. For example, one job training program—no matter how effective—is unlikely to have much effect on the unemployment rate.

One way to somewhat downplay the implied cause-and-effect relationships between individual human service programs and social indicators is to identify groups, or packages, of human service programs that all address the same social indicator. This grouping approach is proposed by the Arizona Self-Sufficiency Matrix (*Arizona Self-Sufficiency Matrix*, 2005). The various human service programs that the Arizona Department of Economic Security provides are to be related to 22 self-sufficiency indicators. Examples of some of the indicators are shown in Table 6.5.

Despite the risks of using social indicators as final outcome performance measures, the comments made in Chapter 3 about the importance of the link between performance measures and identified social problems still apply. Performance measures *should* say something

Table 6.5 Sample Items From the Arizona Self-Sufficiency Matrix

Domain	1	2	3	4	5
Income	No income	Inadequate income and/or spontaneous or inappropriate spending	Can meet basic needs with subsidy; appropriate spending	Can meet basic needs and manage debt without assistance	Income is sufficient, well managed; has discretionary income and is able to save
Employment	No job	Temporary, part time, or seasonal; inadequate pay, no benefits	Employed full time; inadequate pay; few or no benefits	Employed full time with adequate pay and benefits	Maintains permanent employment with adequate income and benefits
Shelter/ Housing	Homeless or threatened with eviction	In transitional, temporary, or substandard housing; and/or current rent/mortgage payment is unaffordable (over 30% of income)	In stable housing that is safe but only marginally adequate	Household is in safe, adequate, subsidized housing	Household is in safe, adequate, unsubsidized housing
Food	No food or means to prepare it. Relies to a significant degree on other sources of free or low-cost food	Household is on food stamps	Can meet basic food needs, but requires occasional assistance	Can meet basic food needs without assistance	Can choose to purchase any food household desires
Childcare	Needs child care but none is available/ accessible and/or child is not eligible	Child care is unreliable or unaffordable, inadequate supervision is a problem for childcare that is available	Affordable, subsidized childcare is available, but limited	Reliable, affordable child care is available; no need for subsidies	Able to select quality child care of choice

about, or relate to, identified social problems, but that does not necessarily imply that a particular human service program is expected to have any impact on the overall social indicators of the community- or state-level social problems. These are two very different issues.

It is, in fact, for the purpose of keeping these issues separate that the focus of this book is on programs and not on agencies or communities. We cannot make any assumptions about cause-and-effect relationships when the unit of analysis is either agency or community. As has been pointed out, it is sometimes even a stretch to make cause-and-effect assumptions about a program, but much more control exists when program is the unit of analysis.

Outcome Performance Measures and Programs of Services

In Chapter 1 and again in Chapter 4, the topic of programs of services was discussed. We suggested that in developing and reporting intermediate output performance measures (units of service) for programs of services, it may be preferable to use separate intermediate outputs for each service or component. This approach, it was argued, has the benefit of providing more comprehensive and detailed pictures of programs of services. Adult day care was used as an example.

When developing and reporting outcome performance measures (either intermediate or final) for programs of services, however, the approach of using separate outcome measures for each service or component is not recommended. Outcome performance measures should be developed for programs of services as a whole and not for their individual services or components. For most programs of services, an individual service or component by itself is not really expected to achieve a quality-of-life change in clients. Rather, it is the *combined effect* of the various services or components that is designed to bring about changes.

Continuing with the example of an adult day care program, an outcome performance measure might be the number of at-risk older persons prevented from being prematurely institutionalized. Individually, none of the services or components of adult day care (transportation, meals, socialization and recreation, health, and others) can reasonably be expected to prevent premature institutionalization of at-risk older persons. But acting together as a program of services, adult day care can accomplish this objective.

Assessing the Four Types of Outcome Performance Measures

An assessment of each of the four types of outcome performance measures will be made as each type is introduced: numeric counts (Chapter 7), standardized measures (Chapter 8), level of functioning scales (Chapter 9), and client satisfaction (Chapter 10). The assessment is based on seven criteria (utility, validity, reliability, precision, feasibility, cost, and unit cost reporting) suggested by previous research specifically relating to outcome performance measurement in human service programs (Kettner & Martin, 1993; Kettner et al., 2008; Kuechler et al., 1988; R. Millar & Millar, 1981; Nurius & Hudson, 1993; Rossi, Lipsey, & Freeman, 2004; Tatara, 1980). These seven criteria are summarized in Table 6.6.

Utility refers to the extent to which the information generated by a particular type of outcome performance measure is considered useful and relevant to stakeholders (R. Millar & Millar, 1981; Nurius & Hudson, 1993). If stakeholders believe that the outcome performance measures adopted by a human service program do not provide useful effectiveness accountability information, then the resulting data will simply be ignored. Utility may well be the most important of the seven criteria in selecting outcome performance measures (Kuechler et al., 1988).

Validity refers to the extent to which a particular type of outcome performance measure really measures what it purports to measure (Rossi et al., 2004). Validity is related to cause-and-effect relationships between human service programs and outcome performance measures. Sometimes, outcome performance measures may actually be measuring extraneous variables such as the influence of a new manufacturing plant opening in a community, or even the well-known Hawthorne effect, rather than the actual results, impacts, and accomplishments of human service programs. The less susceptible an outcome performance measure is to being influenced by extraneous factors other than a human service program, the more valid the measure is.

Reliability refers to the extent to which a particular type of outcome performance measure produces the same results repeatedly (Rossi et al., 2004). As a general rule, the more standardized the outcome performance measure, the more reliable it is.

Precision refers to the extent to which a type of outcome performance measure captures incremental (either quantitative or qualitative) changes

Table 6.6   Criteria for Assessment of Outcome Performance Measures

Criterion	Meaning	Example
Utility	Data generated is useful and relevant to stakeholders	Mastery of selected skills by preschoolers vs. attendance
Validity	The extent to which a performance measure measures what it purports to measure	Hiring and retention in a job vs. a referral for a job interview
Reliability	The extent to which a performance measure produces the same results repeatedly	Homeless consistently remaining in permanent housing after placement vs. return to homelessness
Precision	The extent to which a performance measure captures incremental changes	The use of a 5-point self-sufficiency scale vs. a "yes" or "no" response
Feasibility	The extent to which outside factors may hinder or prevent the use of a measure	The effects of religious training on abstention would be politically difficult to determine
Cost	Start-up and maintenance costs	The use of existing data currently being collected vs. purchasing a standardized scale
Unit cost reporting	The ability of a performance measure to generate cost-per-outcome data	The cost of 12 units of successful counseling vs. the cost of services with no measure of effectiveness

in the quality of life of clients. Precision is directly related to the level of measurement used by an outcome performance measure. Interval level data are more precise than ordinal data. Ordinal data are more precise than nominal data.

Feasibility refers to the extent to which political, ethical, administrative, personnel, or other factors may hinder or prevent the use of a particular type of outcome performance measure (R. Millar & Millar, 1981). The issue here is whether a proposed outcome performance measure is practical. For example, and as a general rule, the more administrative processing time required by a particular type of outcome performance measure, the less feasible it becomes because of demands on staff time.

Cost refers to the start-up and maintenance costs of a particular type of outcome performance measure in relation to the other types (R. Millar & Millar, 1981).

Unit cost reporting refers to the ability to generate cost per outcome data (Kettner & Martin, 1993; Kettner et al., 2008). Outcome performance measures developed with the expectation of satisfying service efforts and accomplishments reporting (GASB, 1993) must be capable of reporting costs per unit of outcome. Some types of outcome performance measures, such as numeric counts, lend themselves more readily to this type of cost analysis than do others.

Each type of outcome performance measure (numeric count, standardized measures, level of functioning scales, and client satisfaction) is rated on each of these seven criteria using a *high, medium, low* scale. The selection of what type or types of outcome performance measures may be best suited to an individual human service program involves not only an individual assessment of all seven criteria but also an assessment of trade-offs between criteria. For example, a human service program might decide on a little less validity and reliability for significantly less cost.

This chapter has provided a general introduction to the topic of outcome performance measures. Chapter 7 will now examine in detail the first of the four major types of outcome performance measures: numeric counts.

Seven

Numeric Counts

Introduction

Numeric counts are the first of the four major types of outcome performance measures to be discussed in detail. Numeric counts resemble output performance measures and outputs with quality dimensions, but with important differences. Because of their similarity in appearance, numeric counts represent a natural bridge to a detailed discussion of outcome performance measures.

What Are Numeric Counts?

Numeric counts were the first type of outcome measures employed in the human services (R. Millar & Millar, 1981). Numeric counts are *simple counts of the number or proportion of clients achieving a quality-of-life change.* One of the most commonly recognized numeric counts comes from the field of education: *graduation rates.* Graduation rates, from elementary school to college, are usually expressed as either a simple count (the number of students graduating) or as a percentage (the proportion of students graduating).

Numeric counts possess two characteristics that set them apart from other types of outcome performance measures. First, they represent simple "head counts" of how many clients achieve a quality-of-life change as a result of a human service program. Second, they are dichotomous (yes/no) measures in which a quality-of-life change either occurs or does not occur for a given client (Kettner, Moroney, & Martin, 2008). Varying degrees of outcome, either quantitative or qualitative, are not captured by numeric counts.

Numeric counts are critical events (conditions, statuses, behaviors, functions, attitudes, feelings, or perceptions) that clients experience as the result of a human service program. Numeric counts can reflect either a desirable event (an unemployed person becoming employed or a child in foster care achieving permanency) or an undesirable event (a client reusing drugs or a juvenile being rearrested). Because a numeric count is by definition "a quality-of-life change," an undesirable outcome (e.g., recidivism) is generally reported as the number or proportion of clients who do not manifest the undesirable condition, status, behavior, and so on. For example, using an undesirable condition like recidivism would more appropriately take the form of the number or proportion of clients who do not recidivate.

Examples of Numeric Counts

Table 7.1 illustrates the use of numeric counts as outcome performance measures for three human service programs: information and referral, home-delivered meals, and counseling. The examples include the use of numeric counts as both intermediate and final outcomes.

Table 7.1   Examples of Numeric Count Outcome Performance Measures

Human service program	Numeric count outcome performance measures

Information and referral
  a. Intermediate outcome performance measure
  b. Final outcome performance measure
	One client receiving assistance
	
	None

Home-delivered meals
  a. Intermediate outcome performance measure
  b. Final outcome performance measure
	One client maintaining good nutrition
	
	One client maintained in own home as part of a program of services

Counseling
  a. Intermediate outcome performance measure
  b. Final outcome performance measure
	One client demonstrating improvement in condition or behavior
	One client demonstrating ability to manage relationships without counseling

Some aspects of Table 7.1 warrant additional explanation. First, no final outcome performance measure is shown for information and referral. A few human service programs, and particularly those that deal with linkage activities (information and referral, specialized transportation for the elderly and disabled), do not lend themselves to the development of final outcome performance measures because, in fact, they are intermediate-related services. The ultimate purposes for which clients use linkage services are simply too varied.

Second, the implied cause-and-effect relationship between the home-delivered meals program and the *final* outcome performance measure shown is tenuous at best. The point about the implied cause-and-effect relationship between a human service program and its outcome performance measures was stressed in Chapter 6, but is worth briefly repeating here. In this case, a home-delivered meals program may assist an elderly or physically disabled individual in maintaining independent living status, but it is hardly sufficient to achieve this desired end state (outcome) by itself. A program of services including—at a minimum—homemaker and visiting nurse as well as home-delivered meals and transportation would more likely be required. Although a home-delivered meals program does not by itself enable a client to live independently in his or her own home, it does contribute to this desirable end state and thus the measure is appropriate for use as a final outcome.

The same point can be made for the *intermediate* outcome performance measure shown for the information and referral (I&R) program. Factors beyond the control of I&R programs affect whether clients ultimately receive services from referral agencies. Nevertheless, I&R programs exist to link clients in need with agencies that can meet those needs. If referrals from an I&R program never result in clients actually receiving assistance, then the program is of little benefit. Consequently, the number of clients who ultimately receive assistance from referrals is an appropriate *intermediate* outcome performance measure for I&R programs even if the implied cause-and-effect relationship is tenuous.

Third, a potentially confusing similarity exists between the numeric counts shown in Table 7.1 and final output performance measures (units of service) and quality performance measures (outputs with quality dimensions) shown in earlier chapters. To highlight the differences, Table 7.2 brings together all three types of performance measures (outputs, quality, and numeric count outcomes) for three human service programs: information and referral, home-delivered meals, and counseling.

Table 7.2   Contrasting Output, Quality, and Numeric Count Outcome
Performance Measures

Human service program	Performance measures	Focus
Information and referral		
a. Intermediate output performance measure (unit of service)	One contact; one referral	Service
b. Output with quality dimension	One appropriate referral	Service
c. Outcome performance measure		
(1) Intermediate	One client receiving assistance	Client
Home-delivered meals		
a. Intermediate output performance measure (unit of service)	One meal	Service
b. Output with quality dimension	One meal delivered hot	Service
c. Outcome performance measure		
(1) Intermediate	One client maintaining good nutrition	Client
(2) Final	One client maintained in own home as part of a program of services	Client
Counseling		
a. Intermediate output performance measure (unit of service)	One hour	Service
b. Output measure with quality dimension	One hour with counselor of record	Service
c. Outcome performance measure		
(1) Intermediate	One client demonstrating improvement in condition or behavior	Client
(2) Final	One client no longer in need of counseling	Client

Table 7.2 shows that output, quality, and outcome performance measures
really do measure different dimensions of a human service program. The
numeric count *outcome* performance measures for all three human service
programs have a *client focus,* whereas the *output* and *quality* performance

measures have a *service focus.* The output performance measures are designed to capture information about how much service is provided by each program. The quality performance measures are designed to capture information about the quality of the service provided by each program. The numeric count outcome performance measures are designed to provide information on the results, accomplishments, or impacts of each program as measured by client quality-of-life changes. Some additional examples of numeric count outcome performance measures commonly used in human service programs are illustrated in Table 7.3.

One feature of Table 7.3, the definitions of the outcome performance measures, warrants some additional discussion. All of the outcome performance measures illustrated in Table 7.3 need to be operationally defined. This is not an unusual situation. For example, the outcome performance measure for job training services is *one person placed in unsubsidized employment.* The term "unsubsidized employment" needs to be operationally defined, perhaps "one person whose salary and benefits are paid entirely by his or her employer." Otherwise, different agency

Table 7.3   Examples of Outcome Performance Measures for Human Service Programs

Human service program	Numeric count outcome performance measure
Job training	One person placed in unsubsidized employment
Child welfare	One child achieving permanency
Adult day care	One elderly person maintained in a safe environment
Head Start/voluntary Pre-K	One child ready to start kindergarten
Case management	One case successfully closed
Case management training	One individual successfully completing training
Homeless services	One person who is no longer homeless
Socialization/recreation for the elderly	One elderly person no longer socially isolated

staff may collect different data based on different understandings of what constitutes "unsubsidized employment." The same issue exists for case management services. We can easily determine what a case closing means, but what does "successful" mean? What circumstances constitute a successful case closure? For Head Start/voluntary Pre-K services, what is meant by "ready to start kindergarten"? In this case, it may mean that a pre-schooler has taken and passed one or more standardized tests. As always, stakeholders must agree on the definitions.

The Preference for Numeric Counts

Numeric counts are the outcome performance measure of choice for government programs, including government human service programs (Zhang, Mikovsky, & Martin, 2006). This preference is based on two factors: (a) collecting data on numeric counts is less complicated and demanding than collecting data on the other three types of outcome performance measures, and (b) numeric counts lend themselves well to the development of unit costs (cost per outcome).

The preference for numeric counts can pose challenges for some human service programs. What happens if a human service program prefers to use standardized measures, level of functioning (LOF) scales, or client satisfaction as an outcome performance measure, but a government funding source requires the reporting of numeric counts? The answer is to find a method of translating these other three types of outcome performance measures into numeric counts. Chapters 8, 9, and 10 contain suggestions on how to perform this translation function.

An Assessment of Numeric Counts

How do numeric counts actually perform as outcome performance measures? Table 7.4 rates numeric counts according to the following criteria: utility, validity, reliability, precision, feasibility, costs, and unit cost reporting. These same criteria will be utilized at the end of Chapter 8 (standardized measures), Chapter 9 (level of functioning scales), and Chapter 10 (client satisfaction).

The *utility* of using numeric counts as an outcome performance measure is rated as *high*. Because so many important classes of stakeholders appear to prefer numeric counts over the other types of outcome performance measures, their ultimate acceptance and use should be considerable.

Table 7.4 Assessment of Numeric Counts as Outcome Performance Measures

Criteria	Rating
Utility	High
Validity	Low to medium
Reliability	High
Precision	Low
Feasibility	High
Cost	Low to medium
Unit cost reporting	High

The *validity* of using numeric counts is rated as *low* to *medium.* The validity of numeric counts depends largely on the extent to which the implied cause-and-effect relationship between an individual human service program and its numeric counts is in fact a real and direct relationship. Do the numeric counts selected for use as outcome performance measures really measure client quality-of-life changes due to participation in human service programs? Or do they measure other factors as well? The same dichotomous yes/no nature that gives numeric counts its high rating on utility poses significant validity problems. It is difficult, and often inaccurate, to reduce client quality-of-life changes to black/white, yes/no categories. An additional validity problem is that numeric count data are frequently generated from agency files and reports that are notoriously incomplete and error prone (R. Millar & Millar, 1981).

The *reliability* of using numeric counts is rated as *high.* The simple dichotomous nature of numeric counts ("yes" the client did achieve a quality-of-life change as defined by the numeric count, or "no" the client did not) should result in a high degree of interrater reliability as well as a high degree of reliability over time.

The *precision* of numeric counts is rated as *low* because, due to its nominal yes/no nature, numeric counts do not deal with varying degrees (either quantitatively or qualitatively) of quality-of-life changes in clients. Thus, numeric counts are significantly less precise than other types of outcome performance measures.

The *feasibility* of using numeric counts is rated as *high*. Numeric counts are relatively easy to develop and interpret. The nature of numeric counts is also such that ethical problems involving client confidentiality are avoided. Administratively, the use of numeric counts—particularly when data that can serve as numeric counts are already being collected—should not pose any significant problems. Finally, political factors should probably work to the advantage of numeric counts, given the strength of the apparent stakeholder support for this type of outcome performance measure.

The *cost* of using numeric counts is rated *low* to *medium*. The cost is low if data that can be used as numeric counts are already being collected, and medium if additional data must be collected and if forms must be redesigned and computer programs altered.

The *unit cost reporting* ability of numeric counts is rated as *high*. Unit cost reporting is in fact tailor-made for numeric counts because they can be expressed as simple nominal counts.

For example, let's assume that a counseling program costs $250,000 to operate for a year. During that same year, 100 clients who were treated no longer require counseling. The cost per outcome is $250,000 /100 = $2,500. It is often more difficult to perform this type of calculation with standardized measures, level of functioning (LOF) scales, and client satisfaction.

On balance, numeric counts tend to hold up well against the assessment criteria. They are easy to use, report, and interpret, but they are less precise and valid than other types of outcome performance measures. In sum, numeric counts score well on the criterion of utility but at the expense of the criteria of precision and validity. If a human service program would rather increase the precision and validity of the outcome performance measures it uses and is willing to sacrifice some utility, standardized measures and/or LOF scales may be the more appropriate choice. In Chapter 8, the discussion focuses on standardized measures, the most valid and precise of the four types of outcome performance measures.

Eight

Standardized Measures

Introduction

As discussed in Chapter 7, numeric counts have many advantages as outcome performance measures. They also have some disadvantages, however. The major disadvantage is the inability of numeric counts to capture varying degrees of client quality-of-life changes.

Some human service programs may need more sensitive outcome performance measures than are provided by the yes/no, black/white nature of numeric counts. For example, struggling families are neither "healthy" nor "dysfunctional." People who abuse alcohol are neither "drinkers" nor "non-drinkers." There are shades of difference on the continuum between these extremes, and these differences can be captured through the use of standardized measures or scales.

What Are Standardized Measures?

Standardized measures are before-and-after tests used to assess quality-of-life changes in clients. Most of us have probably become familiar with standardized measures through the field of education or through tests such as the Stanford-Binet IQ test. Over the past few years there has been considerable controversy about the use of standardized tests to determine promotions and high school graduation. Ideally, standardized measures as used for human service programs are validated, reliable, and normed before-and-after tests used to assess quality-of-life changes in clients. The ways in which they are administered and scored must be consistent. Standardized measures are frequently available for general use but often at a price. Many standardized measures are copyrighted and can be used only with permission of the copyright holder, who frequently charges a fee.

Standardized measures share two common features. First, they generally consist of a set of structured questions designed to solicit information about clients—and sometimes about client families—on conditions, behaviors, attitudes, feelings, intra- or interpersonal functioning, personality development, and other dimensions. Second, they generally include a set of uniform procedures for administration and scoring, usually yielding a single numerical score that is useful in estimating the magnitude, intensity, or degree of the dimension measured (Posavac & Carey, 1997).

The Use of Standardized Measures for Evaluation Versus Research

Most literature and other resource material on standardized measures discuss their value as a research tool. When used for research purposes, findings can be generalized to the client population studied if appropriate use has been made of the data and appropriate tests applied. For research purposes, a determination must be made as to whether the data are considered nominal, ordinal, interval, or ratio (Virginia Tech, 2008). Table 8.1 illustrates these four types of data.

Nominal data refer to simple categories, and when we assign the numbers 0 = male and 1 = female, we are not intending that the numbers themselves have any numerical value. They are simply identifiers for aggregation purposes.

Ordinal data tell us only the order in which findings can be ranked. For example, when clients are asked to rank the services of transportation, meals, and recreation, we may find that meals are the favorite, transportation is second, and recreation third among those who completed the survey, but we do not know that the favorite is twice as popular as the second, or three times as popular as the third. Ordinal data tell us only the order in which findings are to be ranked.

Interval data provide more information. When we can be certain of the meaning of intervals between the numbers 1, 2, 3, and so on, then we know

Table 8.1   Types of Data Produced by Standardized Measures

Type of data	Definition	Example	Use in evaluation
Nominal	Simple categories; numbers are not meaningful	Female = 0; male = 1	Frequently used in collecting numerical program evaluation data
Ordinal	The order in which findings can be ranked	Meal program = most popular; transportation = 2nd; recreation = 3rd	Frequently used in collecting standardized program evaluation data
Interval	Numbers represent a value that is meaningful in terms of the interval between or among them	Physical measurements such as temperature and pulse	Used most often for research purposes; rarely used with standardized measures for evaluation purposes
Ratio	Meaningful relationships can be found between and among sets of findings	Measurement using time or money	Used primarily for research; rarely used for evaluation

that there is significance to the interval and not just to the order. For example, on a thermometer we can say that the interval between 0 and 10 degrees is the same as the interval between 90 and 100 degrees. Most of these scales would involve physical measurements, and it is unlikely that an interval scale would ever be used in any client-completed survey or questionnaire.

The final type of measurement scale is a ratio scale, and with these a meaningful relationship can be assumed between and among different sets of findings. With ratio scales, not only can we say that the difference between 0 and 10 is the same as between 90 and 100, we can also say that each span of 10 points represents a degree of comfort (in the case of the thermometer) or a degree of stress (in the case of appropriate measurement instruments) that is comparable and meaningful. Ratio scales can be used only when the instruments themselves reflect ratio relationships. Most standardized measures used in human services will be nominal or ordinal. It is very rare that interval or ratio measures will be used.

Differences in Standardized Measures

Standardized measures vary in a number of ways. These include (a) the concept measured and whether it has a unidimensional or multidimensional focus, (b) the structure of the scale utilized, (c) the type of respondent, (d) the availability of a clinical cutting score, (e) reliability and validity, and (f) the time, effort, and training needed to administer, score, and interpret results (Bloom, Fischer, & Orme, 2003).

Concept Measured

As Table 8.2 demonstrates, standardized measures vary widely in their focus. For example, a standardized measure can focus on a *population*, such as children, couples, families, adults, or older persons. Other standardized measures focus on *behavior*. Violence, parenting behaviors, job-seeking behaviors, health-related practices, assertiveness, and many other behaviors can be assessed using standardized measures. Another variation is by *attitude*. Attitudes toward self, children, and significant others, for example, are used in counseling clients and client families.

Standardized measures can also have a *problem* focus. Problems such as use of drugs and alcohol, physical health, social dysfunction, and ability to perform basic activities of daily living can all be assessed with standardized measures. In addition, Hudson (1990) has developed a Multi-Problem Screening Inventory (MPSI). Some standardized measures focus on *intrapersonal* or *interpersonal functioning*. Intrapersonal functioning measures include such areas as temperament, self-esteem, thoughts, and depression, whereas interpersonal functioning measures deal with the ability of clients to relate to others, including family members and other social contacts.

A number of standardized measures used with children have *development* as their focus. Others focus on *personality* traits in an effort to produce a personality profile. A number of standardized measures used in job training programs focus on such factors as *achievement, knowledge,* and *aptitude*. Finally, some standardized measures have a *services* focus (e.g., child day care and foster care).

Table 8.2 Focus of Standardized Measures

Focus	Example
Focus	*Example*
Population	A scale for measuring a young child's need for social approval
Problem	A scale for measuring potential for child abuse in parents and prospective parents
Behavior	Scales rating preschool development on several dimensions
Attitude	A scale for measuring attitudes of parents toward child rearing
Intrapersonal	A measure of an individual's belief in ability to attain goals
Interpersonal	A scale for measuring family relationships
Development	A scale for measuring child development
Personality traits	A measure of whether an individual approaches or avoids social interaction
Achievement	A measure of student competence in areas important to career development
Knowledge	A scale for measuring a parent's knowledge of appropriate growth and behavior in children up to age 2
Aptitude	Measures for assessing verbal reasoning, spelling, need for education, and vocation guidance
Services	Measures for assessing child health and nutrition

This listing is meant to be illustrative, not exhaustive, and the categories are not necessarily mutually exclusive. When searching for a particular type of standardized measure, both a literature search and an Internet search are needed to exhaust available options.

Structure of Scale

Standardized measures also vary in the construction of their response scales. The majority of standardized measures use Likert-type scales with response categories indicating frequency. Most of Hudson's (1992) standardized measures use a 7-point scale in which 1 = *none of the time,* 2 = *very rarely,* 3 = *a little of the time,* 4 = *some of the time,* 5 = *a good part of the time,* 6 = *most of the time,* and 7 = *all of the time.* The Marital Communications Skills Rating Scale (Franklin, 1982) offers a scale from 1 to 10 with the single descriptors of inadequate at the low end and adequate at the high end. Other response scales provide brief descriptions at the extremes and ask respondents to select the level that most accurately describes the client. These would all be considered ordinal scales.

Type of Respondent

Standardized measures also differ according to who completes them. Many standardized measures are designed to be completed by clients. For example, Hudson's (1992) personal adjustment measures are completed by clients themselves. These measures help to determine how clients perceive their own behaviors and feelings in a range of areas. Other standardized measures are designed to be completed by professionals or knowledgeable third parties. A number of standardized measures used to assess the ability of older clients to perform activities of daily living can be completed by the client, a caregiver, a relative, or a professional.

Availability of a Clinical Cutting Score

Some standardized measures, such as many of those developed by Hudson (1992), include a *clinical cutting score.* If a client's score on a standard measure is above this threshold, a clinical condition is said to exist. For example, Hudson's (1992) Index of Marital Satisfaction has a clinical cutting score of 30. If a client's score on this standardized measure is above 30, then the client has a clinical condition. This can be very helpful in that it does not require specialized training or education to interpret the score.

Generally, if a client demonstrates either measurable movement toward desirable conditions, status, behaviors, functioning, attitudes, feelings, or perceptions or measurable movement away from undesirable conditions, status, behaviors, functioning, attitudes, feelings, or perceptions, then the client can be said to have experienced a quality-of-life change.

Validity and Reliability

Validity refers to the extent to which a standardized test measures the behaviors the program is designed to change. *Reliability* refers to the extent to which different observers looking at the same phenomenon draw the same conclusions, or different observations over time produce the same results (Posavac & Carey, 1997). Not all standardized measures are equally valid and reliable. In general, the more the measure focuses on objective criteria, the more valid and reliable it will be. Standardized measures should always be checked for validity and reliability as they apply to the population for which they will be used. Many tests have been normed on whites only, males only, females only, adults only, or other specific and perhaps narrowly defined populations.

Time, Effort, and Training Needed to Administer

Some standardized tests require users to have specific training and qualifications in order to administer and score the test. This is most common where the test includes a short answer or essay component and is scored by independent evaluators. Most objective tests are multiple choice and can be scored by computer, but special expertise may be needed to interpret scores.

In a study of the Denver Community Mental Health Questionnaire (Speer, 1977), method of administration, sex, test–retest results, and other factors were investigated. Results indicated troubling differences between methods of administration, effects at follow-up, confounding practice effects, and prominent sex differences on several scales. All of these factors highlight the importance of uniform administration, scoring, and interpretation of scores.

Locating Standardized Measures

Little is available in terms of a single-source Web site for finding scales, and the few general Web sites that exist don't provide much basis for choosing one measure over another. Many of the more popular measures (e.g., the Global Assessment Scale) now have their own Web sites. Probably the best advice for beginning a search is simply to Google "Standardized Scales."

Several universities offer Web sites that are helpful in locating standardized measures. Selected useful reference works that are available online include Tests in Print, Mental Measurements Yearbook, and PsychINFO. For people in the human services, two excellent volumes on standardized measures have been developed by J. Fischer and Corcoran (2007).

Using Standardized Measures as Outcome Performance Measures

The use of standardized measures as outcome performance measures for human service programs requires several actions, as illustrated in Table 8.3. First, the type and number of standardized measures to be used in a human service program must be determined. As is the case with all performance measures, stakeholders should be involved in the selection process.

Second, for standardized measures to produce a meaningful score, all clients must be assessed at the point of entry into the human service program. This score is necessary to establish an individual client baseline profile. Because it is impossible to know which clients will complete treatment and which ones will drop out, a baseline profile must be developed for all clients. Following this assessment, as a third step, clients participate in the human service program.

Fourth, the selected standardized measures are again administered to those clients who complete treatment or receive a full complement of services. If the standardized measures are used to create a treatment profile of a client *immediately* upon completion of treatment or receipt of a full complement of services, the resulting data become intermediate outcome performance measures. When the standardized measures are used to create a post-treatment profile of a client (i.e., at some follow-up point), the resulting data become final outcome performance measures.

Table 8.3   Steps Involved in Using Standardized Measures as Outcome Performance Measures

Step number	Activity
Step 1	Determine the type and number of standardized measures to be used
Step 2	Get a pre-service score on each client on each standardized measure
Step 3	Have the client participate in the program or service
Step 4	Get an immediate post-service score and/or a follow-up post-service score on each client on each standardized measure
Step 5	Compare pre-service score to post-service score

Fifth, a comparison is made between each individual client's baseline profile and the client's treatment profile or post-treatment profile. If a client demonstrates either measurable movement toward desirable conditions, status, behaviors, functioning, attitudes, feelings, or perceptions or measurable movement away from undesirable conditions, status, behaviors, functioning, attitudes, feelings, or perceptions, then the client has experienced a quality-of-life change.

Translating Standardized Measures Into Numeric Counts

Because performance measurement uses program as its unit of analysis, a process must be developed to aggregate individual client standardized measures to the level of human service programs. In considering how to translate standardized measures into numeric counts, it is useful to divide all clients who have completed treatment or received a full complement of services into two groups: (a) clients demonstrating improvement and (b) others. Persons working with data on the clients who demonstrate improvement can develop numeric counts using the following categories:

1. The number of clients who demonstrate measurable improvement

2. The proportion of clients (e.g., $n = 67$) who demonstrate measurable improvement to the total number (e.g., $n = 100$) of clients completing treatment or receiving a full complement of services. In this example, the proportion would be 67%.

3. The number of clients who demonstrate clinical improvement. Clinical improvement can be defined as a client who showed improvement on a clinical cutting score (when one is available) on either the treatment profile or the post-treatment profile.

4. The proportion of clients who demonstrate clinical improvement to the total number of clients who complete treatment or receive a full complement of services

5. The number of clients who achieve a target level of improvement

6. The proportion of clients who achieve a target level of improvement to the total number of clients who completed treatment or received a full complement of services and who had an established target level of improvement

Target level of improvement refers to a level established prior to treatment. Some clients may voluntarily establish a desired target level of improvement for themselves. For example, a married couple may wish to improve their marital satisfaction. Using Hudson's (1992) Index of Marital Satisfaction, the couple may score 50 on the baseline profile and contract with their therapist to reduce the score to 40. If the treatment or post-treatment profile score is 40 or less, the couple can be said to have achieved their target level of improvement. This same approach can also be used with involuntary clients (clients placed into a human service program by the court, a school district, a government agency, a parent, etc.), except that a target level of improvement will be established by someone other than the client.

In human service programs that use multiple standardized measures, numeric count data can be aggregated and reported for each dimension captured by each standardized measure. For example, in an in-home service program for older persons that uses multiple standardized measures, it might be more appropriate to aggregate and report numeric count data that identify client improvement by each standardized measure used (e.g., activities of daily living, social contacts, nutrition, etc.). This approach also has the benefit of communicating more outcome performance measurement data to stakeholders.

An Assessment of Standardized Measures

Table 8.4 provides an assessment of the use of standardized measures as outcome performance measures. As was the case with numeric counts, the criteria of utility, validity, reliability, precision, feasibility, cost, and unit cost reporting are used.

The *utility* of using standardized measures as an outcome performance measure is rated as *low* to *high*. Data generated by standardized measures have *high* utility for stakeholders such as direct service staff and program administrators but low utility for other stakeholders (e.g., citizens, elected officials, and funding sources) who are generally unfamiliar with their use, scoring, and interpretation.

Both the *validity* and *reliability* of standardized measures are rated as *low to high*, depending on the scale. Standardized measures are, ideally, valid and reliable measures, but both of these factors can vary, depending on the particular scale selected. Reliability and validity levels established across many clients may not necessarily hold for any one particular client. In addition, a single standardized measure may be insufficiently sensitive to capture all important client dimensions.

Table 8.4 Assessment of Standardized Measures as an Outcome Performance Measure

Criteria	Rating
Utility	Low to high (depending on stakeholders)
Validity	Low to high (depending on the scale selected)
Reliability	Low to high (depending on the scale selected)
Precision	Medium to high (depending on scale used and number of items)
Feasibility	Low
Cost	High
Unit cost reporting	Low

The *precision* of standardized measures is rated as *medium* to *high*, depending on the individual standardized measure used and the number of items that compose its scale. Some standardized measures are more precise than others. A standardized measure that uses 25 items to assess clinical anxiety, such as Hudson's (1992) scale, will probably be more precise than another standardized measure that uses only 5 or 10 items.

The *feasibility* of using standardized measures is rated as *low.* Many standardized measures must be purchased. Staff must also be oriented and trained in their administration and interpretation. Staff time must also be devoted to their use and scoring as well as to the aggregation of data to the program level.

The *cost* of using standardized measures is rated as *high* for all the reasons stated above. The *unit cost reporting* ability of standardized measures is rated as *low.* In pure form, it is questionable how much relevant unit cost reporting information is supplied by standardized measures. For example, the knowledge that it costs an average of $1,200 to decrease a client's score by one point—or even several points—on a standardized measure is hard to interpret.

Overall standardized scales have a lot to offer, but making good and effective use of them will depend on the problem being assessed, the program being provided, the resources available to the agency, and the purpose or use to which the results will be applied. The use of standardized scales should be given very careful consideration before implementation.

Nine

Level of Functioning (LOF) Scales

Introduction

Standardized measures are good when used for their intended purposes and when a human service program can afford the cost. However, some human service agencies and programs may find that standardized measures do not work for certain populations or problems. The cost of adopting and utilizing a standardized measure may not fit within an agency's budget. It may also be that no standardized measure exists that can assess the particular problem of interest or the population to be assessed. Standardized measures have not been developed for all client quality-of-life changes that are of concern to human service programs. Many of the standardized measures that do exist may be inappropriate for use with certain client populations. For example, a standardized measure designed for use with adults may be inappropriate for use with juveniles or children. Some standardized measures may be "culture bound" and thus inappropriate for use with certain ethnic populations and perhaps with recent immigrants. Finally, some human service programs may simply prefer to develop outcome performance measures that capture the functioning levels of clients before and after treatment as perceived by the local agency. In the situations described above, human service agencies and programs may want to consider the use of level of functioning (LOF) scales.

What Are Level of Functioning (LOF) Scales?

LOF scales are before-and-after assessment instruments, usually designed by agency or program staff for use with a particular target population, that attempt to capture important dimensions of client functioning. Client functioning is broadly defined to include not only functioning but also behaviors and problems. Most LOF scales are designed for use with specific client populations. Some may focus on couples or families. Basically LOF scales can do anything standardized measures can do as far as assessing a client's functioning, behavior, or problem. The difference is that LOF scales are not normed against national samples and their findings cannot be generalized to an entire population.

LOF scales share several common features. They are typically developed at the local agency (or perhaps multi-agency) level by an individual or small group, based on knowledge of and experience with a particular population. As the name implies, they are intended to measure levels of functioning, and therefore must specify degrees from high to low performance or behavior. Sometimes there is a descriptor for every level—sometimes for only certain levels. LOF scales are generally designed to be completed by a case manager or some third party observer rather than by a client. Table 9.1 illustrates an LOF scale with three items that might be used to develop a profile of seniors in a congregate meals program where the objective is to improve, or at least maintain, nutrition and health. Only levels 1, 3, and 5 are described. Levels 2 and 4 are selected if a particular client seems to fall between the descriptors.

LOF scales are usually administered to clients at entry into a human service program and again upon completion of treatment or the receipt of a full complement of services. There may be interim measures as well. LOF scales, like standardized measures, are administered in this before-and-after fashion to create a baseline profile of a client at entry and a post-treatment profile (intermediate outcome performance measure) upon completion of treatment or receipt of a full complement of services. Client profiles, based on LOF scales, may also be used to develop and adjust treatment.

Principles in Designing LOF Scales

The principles that apply to standardized measures, as well as any good measurement instrumentation in general, also apply to designing LOF scales (Babbie, 2005; Bickman & Rog, 2009; Rossi, Lipsey, & Freeman, 2004). These principles are discussed in the following sections under the headings

Table 9.1   Level of Functioning (LOF) Scales for Use in a Congregate Meals
Program for Older Persons

Circle the most appropriate response.

1. **Physical appearance**   1   2   3   4   5

   Level 1: Lack of concern or awareness of physical appearance; personal
   hygiene and clothing neglected
   Level 3: Verbalizes concern about appearance; some assistance required
   Level 5: Careful attention to appearance and personal hygiene is evident

2. **Consumption of meals**   1   2   3   4   5

   Level 1: Consumes 1/3 or less of meal provided
   Level 3: Consumes approximately 1/2 of meal provided
   Level 5: Consistently consumes entire meal; may request seconds

3. **Weight**   1   2   3   4   5

   Level 1: Grossly overweight or underweight according to ideal weight for
   age and body type
   Level 3: Overweight or underweight but motivated to change condition
   Level 5: Maintaining appropriate weight for age and body type

---

of (a) developing a conceptual framework, (b) developing descriptors,
(c) respondent considerations, and (d) constructing LOF scales.

Developing a Conceptual Framework

Well-designed LOF scales are rooted in knowledge of theory, research,
and practice about a human service program and the client population
served. Any time clients are observed and rated, it is important that the
dimensions of functioning on which the rating is based and the *descriptors*
used to anchor the points on the scale be based on an understanding of
the program, the client population served, and the social problem.
Kettner, Moroney, and Martin (2008) identify nine points to be considered
in understanding and analyzing a problem:

1. What is the nature of the situation or condition?

2. How are the terms being defined?

3. What are the characteristics of those experiencing the condition?

4. What is the scale and distribution of the condition?

5. What social values are being threatened by the existence of the condition?

6. How widely is the condition recognized?

7. Who defines the condition as a problem?

8. What is the etiology of the problem?

9. Are there ethnic and gender considerations? (pp. 45–49)

To cite a simplified example, in rating the functioning of children in a day care program, a casual observer might be tempted to construct LOF scales that focus exclusively on disruptive and acting-out behavior. Knowledge of child behavior, however, would make it readily evident that the withdrawn and quiet child who displays little affect may well depict the more serious problem.

Input into the development of LOF scales by program staff, administrators, and other stakeholders (e.g., citizens, funding sources, advocacy groups, etc.) is important but is no substitute for a sound knowledge of the theoretical, research, and practice literature. Table 9.2 illustrates three items on an LOF scale that might be used to rate the interactive behaviors of children in a day care program. These three items (*socialization*, *participation*, and *conversation*) attempt to demonstrate the incorporation of a theoretical and research-based understanding of the social and interpersonal behaviors important to children.

Developing Descriptors

There are three important considerations in the development of descriptors for LOF scales. First, they should describe observable dimensions of client functioning. Second, they should discriminate between different levels of client functioning. Third, they should ideally reflect client behaviors (Labaw, 1980).

One option is to simply scale responses. A five-point scale might use the responses of excellent, very good, good, fair, and poor (Fowler, 2009). One drawback of this kind of scale is that respondents may differ in their understandings of what the descriptors mean. Excellent to one observer might mean good to another, and interrater reliability can be affected. Secondly, these types of descriptors do not provide as much detail as

Table 9.2 Level of Functioning Scales Used to Rate Interactive Behaviors in a Child Day Care Program

---

Circle the most appropriate response.

1. **Socialization**   1   2   3   4   5

   Level 1: Is withdrawn; stays alone; neither voluntarily talks to nor interacts with staff or other children; demonstrates no interest in any interpersonal relationships

   Level 3: Must be encouraged to interact with staff or other children; demonstrates minimal interest in interpersonal relationships

   Level 5: Is outgoing and skillful at building relationships with staff and other children

2. **Participation**   1   2   3   4   5

   Level 1: No participation in activities provided; refuses to participate under any circumstances

   Level 3: Will participate in activities with encouragement

   Level 5: Actively participates and encourages others

3. **Conversation**   1   2   3   4   5

   Level 1: Does not initiate or respond to any conversation with other children or staff

   Level 3: Expresses desire to talk with others but engages in limited verbal interaction

   Level 5: Is highly conversant and enjoys talking with other children and staff

---

those that spell out observable behaviors. This may result in less accurate ratings. Nevertheless, scaled responses are very common and there may be good reasons to use them. Table 9.3 illustrates scaled responses.

LOF scales are generally more accurate when each descriptor describes a level of client functioning that can be determined through direct observation. Descriptors should be written using simple, unambiguous, and verifiable statements. Respondents who complete LOF scales should not be expected to speculate about a client's level of functioning.

To the extent possible, LOF descriptors should be behaviorally oriented. For example, if an LOF scale is used to assess clients on the level of family

Table 9.3   Scaled Responses Used in an LOF Scale

		Poor	Fair	Good	Very good	Excellent
Community involvement	Client and family are involved in community activities in school, church, and civic affairs.					
Education	Client and family members value education and all plan to go as far as they can to achieve their greatest potential.					

harmony/discord, the designers of the scale might be tempted to use a term such as *dysfunctional* as a descriptor. The individuals who actually complete the scales, however, may differ in their interpretation of the meaning of dysfunctional. Consequently, it is preferable to describe behaviors, such as the number of arguments or disagreements per day, or the methods used to resolve disagreements. Behaviorally oriented descriptors remove the need to make evaluative judgments or interpretations and thus increase reliability. As a general rule, the fewer the number of adjectives used in a descriptor, the more consistent will be the meaning attributed to the descriptor. The LOF scales depicted in Table 9.4 provide examples of the use of simple, straightforward language in behavioral terms.

Another important consideration in the development of LOF scales is accuracy. A typical LOF scale will contain points that range across a wide spectrum of client functioning from severely problematic to great strength and stability. Within this range, LOF scale points should allow for as accurate a depiction of each *individual* client as possible, yet at the same time they should also produce relatively homogeneous *groupings*. The California Department of Community Services and Development (1998) attempted to accomplish this with groupings of clients under the

Table 9.4   An Example of the Use of Observable Terms in the Construction of a Level of Functioning (LOF) Scale

	Household management
Level 1	Basic household maintenance functions such as shopping, budgeting, doing dishes, making meals, doing laundry and house cleaning are not planned or managed at all—simply left to be done by the person who is faced with the need or crisis.
Level 3	Some basic household maintenance functions are assigned and carried out, but many are left unassigned and undone. The resulting disruption acts as a barrier to independent functioning.
Level 5	Household functions are planned, managed, and carried out. The ability to handle household maintenance functions is a family strength.

headings of (1) In crisis, (2) Vulnerable, (3) Stable, (4) Safe, and (5) Thriving. Eleven different dimensions (including housing, employment, education, etc.) were used to develop a profile of all clients. Each dimension included a descriptor that allowed as much individualization as possible, while still allowing for groupings under the designated headings. Table 9.5 depicts the descriptors for Shelter.

Respondent Family Considerations

Well-designed LOF scales should be written with the respondent in mind. The term *respondent* generally refers to a person who provides information about him- or herself. In the case of LOF scales, however, the term *respondent* typically refers to a professional staff member who completes the scales on the basis of knowledge and direct observation of a client. Fowler and Cosenza (2009) point out that there are four basic characteristics of questions and answers that are fundamental to a good measurement process:

1. Questions need to be consistently understood.

2. Respondents need to have access to the information required to answer the question.

3. The way in which respondents are asked to answer the question must provide an appropriate way to report what they have to say.

4. Respondents must be willing to provide the answers called for in the question. (p. 376)

Only three ways exist for a respondent to know something about a client: (a) by observing a client directly, (b) by asking a client about her- or himself, and (c) by getting information about a client from a third party (Nurius & Hudson, 1993). In using LOF scales, particular attention should be paid to the length of time a respondent is expected to know a client

Table 9.5   California Level of Functioning Scale Rating Family Shelter

	Shelter
Thriving	Family has a number of housing options and is able to live in stable housing of choice without subsidy. Household budget accommodates housing costs without undue strain on overall family finances.
Safe	Family's housing options are very limited, and family may not be in housing of choice. However, housing is safe and adequate for family size, and tenure is stable. Family can afford housing without subsidy and without compromising with respect to other basic family needs.
Stable	Family is in stable housing that is safe but only marginally adequate either because it is affordable only with the assistance of a subsidy or because its size, location, or condition does not fully meet family's needs.
Vulnerable	Family is living in housing that is transitional or temporary, or unstable. The housing situation is (a) not intended to be permanent (shelter, transitional housing, staying with friends), (b) inadequate due to health or safety problems or overcrowding, or (c) unaffordable—family cannot pay rent and eviction is a possibility.
In crisis	Family is homeless, or it is nearly homeless because (a) housing conditions are so poor as to threaten the health or safety of family members, or (b) eviction is in progress. Family does not have the means to resolve the crisis without outside assistance.

before completing the scale, the type and sources of information about the client that are available to the respondent, and the amount of information required by the respondent to make an accurate assessment of the client. For example, if a respondent is attempting to assess a client's level of family harmony/discord, simply asking a client (especially in a first interview) is unlikely to produce an accurate assessment. If time is allowed for the respondent to develop a professional relationship with the client and to meet and become familiar with other family members, the accuracy of the response will probably increase. This means, of course, that for some behaviors an assessment cannot be made prior to services being provided. Professional judgments sometimes must be made in the interest of compiling a more accurate profile.

In the guidelines for the completion of LOF scales, respondents should be encouraged to make planned, formal observations, either in a client's home, in a natural setting in the community, or in the observer's office. A time-tested set of guidelines for making research-based observations that are useful in thinking about the completion of LOF scales on the basis of direct observation of clients was developed by Epstein and Tripodi (1977).

What Is to Be Observed?

The respondent should be familiar with the LOF scales to be used and should be prepared to focus on a set of expected client behaviors that reflect the areas of functioning under study. If the data are to be gathered through an interview, behavioral referents will be useful in clarifying for the client what is meant by the question.

Site of the Observation

Clients may exhibit different behaviors and give different responses depending on the setting in which the LOF scales are administered. For this reason, respondents should be consistent in the selection of settings for observations. Using multiple settings with the same client may result in differences in observations that have more to do with the setting than with the client.

Frequency of the Observations

In the interest of standardization and reliability, it is important to establish a set number of observations that a respondent uses as a basis for completing an LOF scale. In a residential treatment center, children are generally available for many observations each day. In contrast, couples receiving marriage counseling are typically available once a week for an hour. For the sake of consistency, a set number and type of observations should be specified in the training and preparation of respondents.

Avoiding Influencing the Observation Situation

Objectivity is critical in completing LOF scales. The respondent should make every attempt to be neutral and not influence the observation.

Interjecting comments intended to help a client struggle through a difficult part of an interview or to temper feelings such as anger may result in a less accurate observation.

Reliability of the Observation

Whenever possible, a set of procedures should be established for the completion of LOF scales. The purpose of the procedures is to ensure that the administration of LOF scales varies as little as possible between respondents and from client to client. The procedures should include instructions on the expected number and types of observations on which the LOF scales are to be based, the recommended site(s) of the observation(s), what clients can be told about the LOF scales, what the respondent is hoping to accomplish, and other factors that will help to ensure greater uniformity. Respondents should also be reminded of the factors of boredom and fatigue and a tendency to take the procedures for granted through time. The result can be carelessness and a decline in both the reliability of the process and the accuracy of the resulting data.

Constructing LOF Scales

The actual construction of LOF scales should be carried out by an individual or a small group. Everyone involved in the development should be knowledgeable about the human service program, the client population served, and the social problem addressed. All development of LOF scales should include a plan to have a draft of the scale reviewed by stakeholders representing all relevant groups. The actual development of LOF scales often requires multiple preliminary drafts, thereby affording ample opportunity for feedback, changes, additions, deletions, and corrections. The following steps are typically used to produce good, usable LOF scales:

Step 1: Select the Functions to Be Rated

This is a crucial step because the functions selected form the basis for what will eventually become the outcome performance measures for the human service program. All the functions identified should be capable of changing as the result of a client participating in the human service program.

At this step, it is also necessary to ensure that each identified function is separate and distinct from the others and that no individual function is made up of multiple dimensions. For example, many senior center programs deal with both socialization (interacting with other seniors) and recreation (relaxing and enjoying an activity). These components represent two distinct functions and need to be measured separately by developing at least two separate LOF scale items, one or more dealing with each function.

Step 2: Select the Number of Points on the Scale

Typically, an odd number of points is selected to ensure a high point, a low point, and a midpoint. The midpoint on an LOF scale can be described as that precarious balancing point at which the client can go either way. With appropriate and timely intervention, the client may show improvement. With neglect, the client may deteriorate.

LOF scales can have as few as 3 points or as many as 10 (Fowler, 2009). Three points may provide insufficient variability for measurement purposes. Conversely, LOF scales with 10 points or more may provide too much variability, thereby reducing interrater reliability. Fowler and Cosenza (2009) point out that there are limits to the extent to which people can use scales to provide meaningful information. Most studies show that little new information is provided by more than 10 categories.

Step 3: Write the Descriptors

In most instances, performance measurement is designed to produce ordinal data. This means that the descriptors for each item on an LOF scale must clearly represent levels from low to high functioning. Descriptors should be based on typical, observable, verifiable client behaviors. Inadequate wording, poor wording, and poorly defined terms should be avoided. This is often a challenge because what is clear wording to some may not be clear to others. Relative terms such as "adequate," "dysfunction," and "harmony" may have different meanings to different respondents. Descriptors should also cover only one behavior. An item that asks the respondent to rate a client's level of depression and antisocial feelings, for example, should be separated into two different items.

Step 4: Field-Test the LOF Scales

Once good working drafts of the LOF scales to be used in a human service program have been developed, they should be circulated among staff members for use in field testing with clients. On the basis of the field test, staff suggestions, additions, deletions, and corrections are incorporated. Final working drafts of LOF scales are then ready for reliability testing.

Step 5: Test Reliability of the LOF Scales

Reliability testing involves several respondents completing the LOF scales for the same clients. Case scenarios can be used either in written form, on video, or in a role-play simulation. A simple index of interrater reliability can then be computed on the basis of the percentage of agreements. An index of 70% to 80% interrater agreement is generally regarded as fairly high (Epstein & Tripodi, 1977).

Translating LOF Scales Into Numeric Counts

Because performance measurement uses programs as its unit of analysis, LOF scale data—like those produced by standardized measures—must be translated into numeric counts for reporting purposes. The same process used for standardized measures can be used for LOF scales. Clients can be thought of as falling into two groups: (a) those demonstrating improvement and (b) other. Through the use of this approach, numeric count data can be collected, aggregated, and reported using such categories as (a) the number of clients demonstrating improvement and (b) the proportion of clients demonstrating improvement to the total number of clients who complete treatment or receive a full complement of services. Fewer options exist in translating LOF scales into numeric counts than exist for standardized measures. This is because LOF scales generally do not have either clinical cutting points or target levels of improvement.

An Assessment of LOF Scales

Table 9.6 provides a summary assessment of LOF scales. Again, the seven criteria of utility, validity, reliability, precision, feasibility, cost, and unit cost reporting ability are used.

The *utility* of LOF scales as an outcome performance measure is rated as *low* to *high*. Like standardized measures, LOF scales have *high* utility for some stakeholders such as program staff and agency administrators but *low* utility for other stakeholders (e.g., citizens, elected officials, and funding sources) who may be unfamiliar with their use, scoring, and interpretation.

The *validity* of LOF scales is rated as *medium* to *high*. Well-designed LOF scales should measure what they purport to measure. Consequently, face validity should be high. Validity can be enhanced through time by the systematic verification that each descriptor used on an LOF scale measures what it purports to measure.

The *reliability* of LOF scales is rated as *medium* to *high*. LOF scales can be continuously tested and modified to increase both interrater and intrarater reliability. As scales are used through time and staff become more experienced in making judgments about level of client functioning, reliability is typically increased (Epstein & Tripodi, 1977; Kuechler et al., 1988).

Table 9.6   An Assessment of Level of Functioning Scales as an Outcome Performance Measure

Criteria	*Rating*
Utility	Low to high
Validity	Medium to high
Reliability	Medium to high
Precision	Medium
Feasibility	Low
Cost	High
Unit cost reporting	Low

The *precision* of LOF scales is rated as *medium*. Although LOF scales are more precise than numerical counts, they tend to be less precise than standardized measures. If precision is a priority concern, additional points and descriptors can be added to LOF scales. A point of diminishing utility can be reached, however, when additional points and descriptors add little to the precision of LOF scales.

The *feasibility* of LOF scales is rated as *low*. The use of LOF scales—like standardized measures—requires a considerable commitment of staff, time, and money. Program staff may also find the complexity of LOF scales intrusive, a problem that can hinder their use.

The *cost* of LOF scales is rated as *high*. Costs include staff costs, and perhaps consultant time, to develop the LOF scales and additional staff time and costs to assess clients using the LOF scales. In addition, the supervisory, management, and administrative costs involved in collecting, aggregating, and reporting the resulting data can be considerable.

Finally, the *unit cost reporting* ability of LOF scales is rated as *low*. LOF scales suffer from the same problems of interpretation as standardized measures. How does one interpret the following unit cost: $1,200 to move one client one point on a particular LOF scale? It *can* be interpreted but it will probably be more meaningful to some stakeholders than to others.

In summary, level of functioning (LOF) scales can be very useful in performance measurement if they are developed and used carefully and professionally. In the next chapter we turn our attention to the fourth type of performance measure, client satisfaction.

Ten

Client Satisfaction

Introduction

The last of the four major types of outcome performance measures to be discussed is client satisfaction. Because much of the introductory groundwork on client satisfaction was presented in Chapter 5 dealing with quality performance measures, the discussion here is considerably abbreviated. This brevity should not be construed as reflecting negatively on the relative importance of client satisfaction as compared with the other three types of outcome performance measures.

Using Client Satisfaction as an Outcome Performance Measure

In addition to serving as a quality performance measure, as was demonstrated in Chapter 5, client satisfaction can also be used as an intermediate outcome performance measure. As a general rule, and in actual practice, client satisfaction is not generally utilized as a final outcome performance measure. Client satisfaction becomes an outcome performance measure when clients are asked to self-report about quality-of-life changes they experienced through participation in human service programs.

The actual process of using client satisfaction as an outcome performance measure is relatively straightforward—provided a human service program already collects and reports quality performance data

based on consumer satisfaction surveys. For example, the client satisfaction survey questionnaire that was shown in Table 5.6 could be used
to generate outcome performance measures data by *simply adding one
additional question.*

Continuing with the examples of information and referral, home-
delivered meals, and counseling, Table 10.1 demonstrates how one
additional question on a survey can generate outcome performance
measures data for each of these three human service programs. Because
these three questions ask clients to self-report on quality-of-life changes,
the questions become intermediate outcome performance measures and
the resulting client responses constitute intermediate outcome performance measures data.

Table 10.1   Using a Client Satisfaction Survey to Generate Outcome Performance
Measurement Data

Information and Referral

Question: Has the information and referral program been helpful to you in
accessing needed services?

Very unhelpful	Somewhat unhelpful	Neither helpful or unhelpful	Somewhat helpful	Very helpful
1	2	3	4	5

Home-Delivered Meals

Question: Has the home-delivered meals program been helpful to you in
maintaining your health and nutrition?

Very unhelpful	Somewhat unhelpful	Neither helpful or unhelpful	Somewhat helpful	Very helpful
1	2	3	4	5

Counseling

Question: Has the counseling program been helpful to you in coping with the
stress in your life?

Very unhelpful	Somewhat unhelpful	Neither helpful or unhelpful	Somewhat helpful	Very helpful
1	2	3	4	5

Translating Client Satisfaction Outcomes Into Numeric Counts

Because of the preference of governments at all levels for numeric counts as outcome performance measures, some thought needs to be given to how client satisfaction outcome data can be translated into numeric counts. Fortunately, this process is not difficult. One approach is to simply determine the actual number, or percentage, of clients responding *Somewhat helpful* or *Very helpful* to each question (see Table 10.1). The resulting numeric counts might look something like this:

- 78% of responding clients rate the information and referral program as *Somewhat helpful* or *Very helpful* in accessing needed services.
- 82% of responding clients rate the home-delivered meals program as *Somewhat helpful* or *Very helpful* in enabling them to maintain their health and nutrition.
- 55% of responding clients report that the counseling program was *Somewhat helpful* or *Very helpful* in coping with stress in their lives.

An Assessment of Client Satisfaction

Table 10.2 summarizes the assessment of using client satisfaction as an outcome performance measure. The rating criteria of utility, validity, reliability, precision, feasibility, cost, and unit cost reporting are discussed below.

The *utility* of using client satisfaction as an outcome performance measure is rated as *medium*. Client satisfaction is of interest to a variety of stakeholders. Elected officials, funding agencies (government and foundations), program administrators, and agency administrators are all generally interested in—and concerned about—clients' perceptions of the effectiveness of human service programs. Most stakeholders also recognize the inherent limitations of client satisfaction data.

The *validity* of using client satisfaction as an outcome performance measure is rated as *low* to *medium*. Client satisfaction by its very nature is subjective, and many clients are "involuntary." One can never be sure that clients' assessments of quality-of-life changes are accurate. Nevertheless, clients provide an important perspective on the effectiveness of human service programs that cannot be gained from any of the other three types of outcome performance measures.

Table 10.2   Assessment of Client Satisfaction as an Outcome Performance Measure

Criteria	Rating
Utility	Medium
Validity	Low to medium
Reliability	Medium
Precision	Low
Feasibility	Medium
Cost	Low to high for start-up
Unit cost reporting	High

The *reliability* of using client satisfaction as an outcome performance measure is rated as *medium.* Reliability as it pertains to the use of client satisfaction as an outcome measure is related primarily to the degree of variability in the survey questions used to solicit the data. Reliability can be enhanced by using standardized survey questions that do not vary from client to client or from survey to survey.

The *precision* of using client satisfaction as an outcome performance measure is rated as *low.* Client self-reporting by its very nature is not precise. Asking clients to self-report on their quality-of-life changes incurred as a result of having participated in human service programs is perhaps even less precise.

The *feasibility* of using client satisfaction as an outcome performance measure is rated as *medium.* Although the process of actually collecting data can be cumbersome, the effort required is probably no greater than that required for the other types of outcome performance measures. A caveat here is that feasibility probably declines with time. Tracking down and surveying clients months after they have completed treatment or have received a full complement of services is problematic.

The *cost* of using client satisfaction as an outcome performance measure ranges from *low* to *high.* If a human service program is already collecting client satisfaction data to serve as a quality performance measure, the incremental cost of adding, analyzing, and reporting data on one additional question—or even a few additional questions—should be *low.* If client satisfaction data are not currently collected, start-up costs (including the cost of developing the surveys, surveying clients, and analyzing and reporting the data) will probably be high.

The *unit cost reporting* ability of using client satisfaction as an outcome performance measure is rated as *high.* Outcome performance measures data based on client satisfaction will closely resemble numeric counts (i.e., a specified number or percentage of clients achieving a quality-of-life change).

An Assessment of the Four Types of Outcome Performance Measures

Now that all four types of outcome performance measures have been introduced and discussed, it may be useful to compare and contrast them using the common criteria of utility, validity, reliability, precision, feasibility, cost, and unit cost reporting ability. As Table 10.3 illustrates, each of the four types of outcome performance measures has advantages and disadvantages. For example, standardized measures and LOF scales are rated as more precise, valid, and reliable, but they are also rated as costing

Table 10.3   An Assessment of the Four Types of Outcome Performance Measures

Criteria	Numeric counts	Standardized measures	LOF scales	Client satisfaction
Utility	High	Low to high	Low to high	Medium
Validity	Low to medium	Low to high	Medium to high	Low to medium
Reliability	High	Low to high	Medium to high	Medium
Precision	Low	Medium to high	Medium	Low
Feasibility	High	Low	Low	Medium
Cost	Low to medium	High	High	Low to high
Unit cost reporting	High	Low	Low	High

more. Numeric counts are considered as having more utility and costing less, but they also are considered to be less valid, reliable, and precise. Client satisfaction, by comparison, is more middle of the road, rated *medium* on more criteria than any of the other three.

In the final analysis, it is probably the nature of the human service program itself and the preferences of stakeholders that may ultimately determine which type or types of outcome performance measures are used. Many human service programs may wind up using at least two types, numeric counts and one of the other three.

Eleven

Using Performance Measurement Information

Introduction

One of the major purposes for adopting performance accountability and performance measurement is to improve the performance of human service programs. The use of data and information to improve program performance goes by several names, including data-driven decision making, evidenced-based practices (when the focus is on outcomes), performance management, and others (Myers, Smith, & Martin, 2006; Wye, 2002).

This final chapter demonstrates how performance data and information can be utilized to improve the *planning, monitoring,* and *reporting* of human service programs. For these purposes, a case example is employed. As part of the case study, some initial background information is first provided on the setting (the town), the human service agency, and the programs the agency operates.

The Town

Riverview, Florida, is a town of about 75,000 people with a population that is 62% white, 18% African American, 14% Hispanic, 3% Asian, and 3% Native American. There are three high schools, three junior high schools,

119

and six elementary schools. Major employers are manufacturing and service industries. Unemployment typically runs around 6% to 7%. The Child Protective Services (CPS) unit of the Florida Department of Children and Families (Florida DCF) receives referrals from schools, physicians, day care centers, neighbors, and other sources. CPS deals with the legal aspects of child abuse and neglect, and contracts out investigations, counseling, and other services to local governments and nonprofit agencies.

The Agency and the Human Service Programs

Riverview Family Services (RFS) is a private, nonprofit community-based human services agency that generates revenue from federal, state, and local government grants and contracts; the local United Way; and from its own special fundraising projects. RFS has three programs (Figure 11.1):

1. An *Intensive Case Management* (ICM) program with a supervisor and 10 caseworkers. Each caseworker carries a caseload of approximately 10 cases each.

2. A *Parental Skills Training* (PST) program with a supervisor and 4 contracted trainers.

3. An *Upgrading Employment* (UE) program with a supervisor and 5 employment specialists.

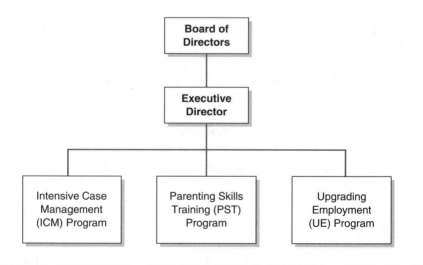

Figure 11.1 Organization Chart for Riverview Family Services

One of RFS's government contracts is with the Florida DCF to provide intensive case management, parenting skills training, and employment services. This contract requires the RFS to serve about 400 families a year. Florida DCF child protective services workers screen and refer cases to RFS.

Case managers in the ICM program meet with their assigned families at least once a week and help them to get their home situation and their finances in order. The PST program receives referrals from CPS workers and conducts 15-week courses covering basic child management skills. During the training, staff also observe the interactions of parents with their children. The UE program is designed to assist clients in securing employment at their highest possible levels given their circumstances. Staff of the UE program provide assistance with resume preparation, scheduling of employment interviews, General Educational Development (GED) diplomas, specialized training programs, and registration for community college courses and other activities.

Planning Using Performance Measures

The main thrust of Chapter 3 was the development and use of logic models to better understand the relationships between and among social or community problems, assumptions about the nature of those problems, the design of human service programs to address the problems, and the elements of performance measurement (outputs, quality, and outcomes). Table 11.1 depicts these relationships for the programs operated by RFS.

Developing Performance Measures and Objectives

One of the most important aspects of human service program planning is arguably the development of output, quality, and outcome performance measures and the establishment of objectives for each. The adoption of output, quality, and outcome performance measures provides the metrics by which program performance will be evaluated. The establishment of objectives makes explicit the levels of performance that the human service program plans to achieve.

Continuing with the case example, each of the three programs provided by RFS needs to develop output, quality, and outcome performance measures and set performance objectives for each. Materials from Chapters 4, 5, and 6 provide the basis for these actions. Before proceeding

Table 11.1   Logic Model Beginning With a Social Problem

Social problem:	Violence against children		
	↓		
Program objectives:	To improve the home management, budgeting, parenting, and employable skills of parents at risk of abusing their children		
	↓		
Assumptions:	At-risk parents are deficient in home management, budgeting, parenting, and/or employable skills, and that with improved skills and the application of these skills they will no longer physically abuse their children		
	↓		
Human service program:	Intensive Case Management (ICM) Parenting Skills Training (PST) Program Upgrading Employment (UE) Program		
	↓		

	Output performance measure	*Quality performance measure*	*Outcome performance measure*
Definitions	Measurements of services provided and completion of all services	Measures of quality of services provided	Demonstrated benefits to those receiving service (results, accomplishments, impacts)

further, it is useful to quickly review the basics on output, quality, and outcome performance measures.

1. **Outputs:** There are two types: *intermediate* and *final.* Intermediate outputs are measures of the volume of service or product produced measured in time, episode, or material units of service. Final outputs are measures of service completion: one client completing treatment or receiving a full complement of services.

2. **Quality:** In Chapter 5, several dimensions of quality were identified:

Accessibility	Courtesy	Performance
Assurance	Deficiency	Reliability
Communication	Durability	Responsiveness
Competency	Empathy	Security
Conformity	Humaneness	Tangibles

Quality is operationalized in performance measurement by selecting at least one of the above quality dimensions and tying it to an intermediate output performance measure or unit of service selected. For example, if reliability is selected as a measure of quality, an intermediate output measure, or unit of service, with a quality dimension might be: "One counseling session starting on time."

3. **Outcomes**: Outcomes are the results, accomplishments, or impacts attributable, at least in part, to the services provided. In Chapter 6, it was pointed out that outcomes in human service programs are generally operationalized as quality-of-life changes in clients. Several types of outcomes, or client quality-of-life changes, were identified: conditions, status, behaviors, functioning, attitudes, and feelings. It was also pointed out that quality-of-life changes can be measured in four ways: numeric counts, standardized measures, level of functioning (LOF) scales, and client satisfaction. Given these reminders, Tables 11.2, 11.3, and 11.4 present the output, quality, and outcome performance measures and objectives for the three programs operated by RFS: (1) intensive case management, (2) parent training, and (3) upgrading employment.

Monitoring Performance

At the weekly executive staff meetings of RFS, the executive director and program supervisors utilize the agency's dashboard system to review the performance of the agency's three programs. A dashboard is an interactive computer system that includes performance measures, metrics, indicators, and links to relevant reports. Dashboards generally provide the ability to "drill down" into performance data and to conduct trend analyses (Zhang, Mikovsky, & Martin, 2006).

Today, most government agencies and many nonprofit human service agencies utilize dashboards to monitor ongoing program performance. For

Table 11.2   Intensive Case Management (ICM) Program Performance Measures and Objectives

---

Output Performance Measures and Objectives

A. Intermediate output performance measure (unit of service)
   – One hour of case manager time (time unit)

B. Intermediate output performance objective
   – To provide 12,500 hours of service

C. Final output performance measure (service completion)
   – One client completing all services specified in the case plan

D. Final output performance objective
   – 275 clients

Quality Performance Measure and Objective

A. Intermediate quality performance measure (reliability)
   – Working with the same case manager throughout the entire episode of service

B. Intermediate quality performance objective
   – 95% quality level

Outcome Performance Measures and Objectives

A. Intermediate outcome performance measure
   – Demonstrated ability to construct and live within a budget (performing at Level 3 or better on LOF scale for behavior)

B. Intermediate outcome performance objective
   – 250 families

C. Final outcome performance measure
   – Demonstrated ability to construct and live within a budget (performing at Level 3 or better on LOF scale for behavior)

D. Final outcome performance objective
   – 210 families

---

example, the U.S. federal government utilizes a dashboard system to track and report on the performance of all executive branch departments and agencies (www.whitehouse.gov/results/agenda/FY08Q3-SCORECARD.pdf). The Florida DCF also uses a dashboard to monitor the performance of all contracted child welfare agencies in the state. Any stakeholder (DCF employee, contract agency, employee, citizen, advocacy group, etc.) can access

Table 11.3 Parent Training (PT) Program Performance Measures and Objectives

---

Output Performance Measures and Objectives

A. Intermediate output performance measure (unit of service)
   – One class meeting (episode unit)

B. Intermediate output performance objective
   – 300 class meetings

C. Final output performance measure (service completion)
   – One client receiving a certificate of completion

D. Final output performance objective
   – 325 clients

Quality Performance Measure and Objective

A. Intermediate quality performance measure (reliability)
   – One scheduled class or meeting starting on time

B. Intermediate quality performance objective
   – 95% quality level

Outcome Performance Measure and Objective

A. Intermediate outcome performance measure
   – Demonstrated mastery of at least 12 parenting skills
     (standardized measure for attitude)

B. Intermediate outcome performance objective
   – 85% of clients

---

the Florida DCF dashboard and review the performance of the child welfare system (http://dcfdashboard.dcf.state.fl.us). Beginning with a map of the state of Florida, stakeholders can drill down to the regional level, to the program level, and to the provider level.

Returning to the case example, a major activity of each weekly staff meeting at RFS is a review of program performance utilizing the agency's dashboard system. Meeting in April, the RFS's management team can review the summary progress of all programs for the first quarter (Jan/Feb/Mar), compare it against performance objectives, and propose any modifications necessary for the coming month (Figure 11.2). Utilizing this approach, the RFS's leadership is engaging in data-driven decision making, evidenced-based practices, and performance management.

Table 11.4   Upgrading Employment (UE) Program Performance Measures and Objectives

---

Output Performance Measures and Objectives

A. Intermediate output performance measure (unit of service)
   – One hour with employment specialist engaged in planned activities (time unit)

B. Intermediate output performance objective
   – 12,000 hours

C. Final output performance measure (service completion)
   – One client completing all the services specified in the employment plan

D. Final output performance objective
   – 275 clients

Quality Performance Measure and Objective

A. Intermediate quality performance measure
   – Client satisfaction (accessibility)

B. Intermediate quality performance objective
   – 95% of clients rate the accessibility of EU program staff as "good or excellent"

Outcome Performance Measure and Objective

A. Final outcome performance measure
   – One client employed for 12 months (numeric count)

B. Final outcome performance objective
   – 150 clients

Reporting Using Performance Measures

The service efforts and accomplishments (SEA) reporting initiative of the Governmental Accounting Standards Board (GASB) was discussed in Chapter 2. Table 11.5 reminds us what is included in an SEA report.

SEA reporting requires a good deal of financial information. Budgeting has not been covered in this book. However, the reader is referred to Kettner, Moroney, and Martin (2008), Chapters 10 and 11, for a thorough discussion of budgeting in human service programs. For the sake of this case example, the Intensive Case Management

Program	Objective	Jan	Feb	Mar	Status
Intensive Case Management (ICM)					
A. Outputs					
– Intermediate (hours)	12,500	1,000	1,110	1,200	◑
– Final (service completions)	275	22	23	25	○
B. Quality					
– Intermediate (% rating the service good or excellent)	95%	95%	95%	95%	○
C. Outcomes					
– Intermediate	250	9	20	18	●
– Final	210	15	18	17	●
Parent Training (PT)					
A. Outputs					
– Intermediate (classes)	300	25	25	25	○
– Final (service completions)	325	28	27	27	○
B. Quality					
– Intermediate (% rating the service good or excellent)	95%	95%	95%	96%	◑
C. Outcomes					
– Intermediate (% of clients achieving the outcome)	85%	87%	86%	85%	○
Upgrading Employment (UE)					
A. Outputs					
– Intermediate (hours)	12,000	1,000	1,050	1,150	●
– Final (service completions)	275	22	23	24	○
B. Quality					
– Intermediate - Intermediate (% rating the service ood or excellent)	95%	90%	90%	92%	○
C. Outcomes					
– Final outcome	150	12	11	10	●

On Schedule ○   Ahead of Schedule ◑   Behind Schedule ●

Figure 11.2 Riverdale Family Services Dashboard Report for April

127

Table 11.5   Service Efforts and Accomplishments Ratios

SEA ratios	Example
1. Efficiency (output measures) a. Cost per unit of service b. Units of service per FTE c. Cost per service completion d. Service completions per FTE	 $27.27 ($750,000/27,500) 1,250 (27,500/22 FTE staff) $3,333 ($750,000/225) 10.23 (225/22)
2. Effectiveness (outcome) measures a. Cost per outcome b. Outcomes per FTE	 6,696.42 (750,000/112) 5.01 (112/22)
3. Interpretations a. The average cost per hour of training is $27.27. b. Each trainer provided an average of 1,250 hours of training. c. The average cost per family completing the training was $3,333. d. Each trainer resulted in 10.23 families completing the training. e. The cost to achieve the outcome of one family not abusing or neglecting its children for a minimum period of 2 years is $6,696.42 f. The average number of outcomes attributable to each trainer is 5.01.	

Note: This table is a reproduction of Table 2.6.

Program is utilized, with a hypothetical budget of $600,000 repre-
senting total program costs. Given this cost figure and the inputs,
program, outputs, quality, and outcomes specified in this case
example, an SEA report for Intensive Case Management might look
something like Table 11.6 and Table 11.7.

Performance Accountability and Performance Measurement

We have now come full circle. This book began with a discussion of logic models and an explanation of how many forces from federal, state, and local governments are converging to require human service agencies and

Table 11.6 An SEA Report for Riverdale Family Services (Part I)

	Service Efforts and Accomplishments	
Program:	Intensive Case Management	
Inputs:	Total program cost	$600,000
	Full time equivalent staff (FTEs)	10
	Hours worked (50 weeks × 40 hours × 10 workers)	20,000 hours
	Client families	400
Outputs:	*Intermediate outputs*	
	Units of service	12,500 direct service hours
	Final outputs	
	Families who completed all services in the case plan	275 families
	Quality outputs	
	Reliability – Working with the same case manager throughout the entire episode of service	245 families
Outcomes:	*Intermediate outcomes*	
	Demonstrated ability to construct and live within a budget as measured by moving up at least one level on the Riverview Income Management scale and performing at least at Level 3, Barely Able to Meet Expenses	250 families
	Final outcome	
	Remaining at Level 3 or above in a 6-month follow-up	210 families

Table 11.7   An SEA Report for Riverdale Family Services (Part II)

Service Efforts and Accomplishments Ratios	
Efficiency measures:	
Cost per unit of service ($600,000/12,500)	$48.00 per unit
Cost per service completion	($600,000/275) $2,181.81
Units of service per FTE (12,500 units/10 FTE)	1,250 units
Service completions per FTE (275/10)	27.5 completions
Effectiveness measures:	
Cost per intermediate outcome ($600,000/250 successes)	$2,400 per successful outcome at completion
Cost per final outcome ($600,000/210 successes at follow-up)	2,857.14 per successful outcome at follow-up
Intermediate outcomes per FTE (250/10)	25
Final outcomes per FTE (210/10)	21

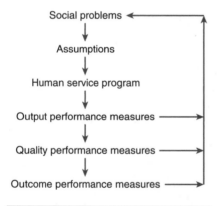

Figure 11.3   The Logic Model Link Between Social Problems, Human Service Programs, and Performance Measures

programs to adopt performance accountability and performance measurement. Each of the elements identified in Figure 11.3 was discussed in detail.

In this 11th and final chapter, we have attempted to briefly illustrate the ways in which performance measurement data can be used. It is our hope that we have been able to make this clear enough that managers of human services programs as well as caseworkers, board members, and all concerned stakeholders can understand and apply the concepts.

References

Ables, P., & Murphy, M. (1981). *Administration in the human services.* Englewood Cliffs, NJ: Prentice-Hall.

Adoption and Safe Families Act of 1997, Pub. L. No. 105-89, 111 Stat. 2115.

American Public Welfare Association. (1980). *A report of the national conference on client outcome monitoring procedures for social services.* Washington, DC: Author.

Anthony, R., & Young, D. (1994). *Management control in non-profit organizations* (5th ed.). Burr Ridge, IL: Irwin.

Anthony, R., & Young, D. (2003). *Management control in non-profit organizations* (7th ed.). Burr Ridge, IL: Irwin.

Arizona self-sufficiency matrix. (2005). Retrieved October 21, 2008, from http://symmetricsolutions.com/ruralazhmis/documents.html

Babbie, E. (2005). *The basics of social research* (4th ed.). Belmont, CA: Wadsworth.

Benveniste, G. (1994). *The twenty-first century organization.* San Francisco: Jossey-Bass.

Bickman, L., & Rog, D. (Eds.). (2009). *Applied social research methods.* Thousand Oaks, CA: Sage.

Bliss, D. (2007). Implementing an outcomes measurement system in substance abuse treatment programs. *Administration in Social Work, 31,* 83–101.

Bloom, M., Fischer, J., & Orme, J. (2003). *Evaluation practice: Guide for the accountable professional* (4th ed.). Boston: Allyn & Bacon.

Bowers, G., & Bowers, M. (1976). *The elusive unit of service.* Washington, DC: U.S. Department of Health, Education, and Welfare, Office of the Secretary, Project SHARE.

Brody, R. (2005). *Effectively managing human service organizations* (3rd ed.). Thousand Oaks, CA: Sage.

California Department of Community Services and Development. (1998). *Background materials for a conversation about use of scales to measure family, community, and agency outcomes.* San Rafael, CA: Author.

Carmeli, A. (2006). The managerial skills of the top management team and the performance of municipal organizations. *Local Government Studies, 32,* 163–176.

Carter, R. (1983). *The accountable agency.* Newbury Park, CA: Sage.

Council on Accreditation. (2008). *PQI: Leaderships endorsement of quality and performance values*. New York: Author. Retrieved July 8, 2008, from www.coastandards.org

Cronbach, L. (1982). *Designing evaluations of educational and social programs*. San Francisco: Jossey-Bass.

Crosby, P. (1985). *Quality without tears: The art of hassle-free management*. New York: Plume.

Deming, W. (1986). *Out of the crisis*. Cambridge, MA: MIT Center for Advanced Engineering Study.

Else, J., Groze, V., Hornby, H., Mirr, R., & Wheetlock, J. (1992). Performance-based contracting: The case of residential treatment. *Child Welfare, 71,* 513–525.

Epstein, I., & Tripodi, T. (1977). *Research techniques for program planning, monitoring, and evaluation*. New York: Columbia University Press.

Fischer, E. (2005). Facing the challenges of outcomes measurement: The role of transformational leadership. *Administration in Social Work, 29,* 35–49.

Fischer, J., & Corcoran, K. (2007). *Measures for clinical practice: A sourcebook* (Vol. 2, 4th ed.). New York: Oxford University Press.

Fowler, F. (2009). *Survey research methods* (4th ed.). Thousand Oaks, CA: Sage.

Fowler, F., & Cosenza, C. (2009). Design and evaluation of survey questions. In L. Bickman & D. Rog (Eds.), *Applied social research methods* (pp. 375–412). Thousand Oaks, CA: Sage.

Franklin, C. (1982). *Gottman couples communication rating scale*. Monograph.

Gallagher, R. (2008). *Accountability in the non-profit sector*. United Way of America. Retrieved February 13, 2008, from www.Unitedway.org/About/accountability_non.cfm

Gilmour, J. (2006). *Implementing OMB's program assessment rating tool (PART)*. Washington, DC: The IBM Center for the Business of Government. Retrieved July 14, 2008, from www.businessofgovernment.org

Government Performance and Results Act of 1993, Pub. L. No. 103–62, 107 Stat. 285.

Governmental Accounting Standards Board. (1993). *Proposed statement of the Governmental Accounting Standards Board on concepts related to service efforts and accomplishments reporting an amendment of GASB concepts statement no. 2*. Norwalk, CT: Author.

Governmental Accounting Standards Board. (2008). *Proposed statement of the Governmental Accounting Standards Board on concepts related to service efforts and accomplishments reporting an amendment of GASB concepts statement no. 2*. Norwalk, CT: Author.

Gunther, J., & Hawkins, F. (1996). *Making TQM work: Quality tools for human service organizations*. New York: Springer Publishing Company.

Hatry, H., & Wholey, J. (1994). *Toward useful performance measurements: Lessons learned from pilot performance plans under the Government Performance & Results Act*. Washington, DC: National Academy of Public Administration.

Hudson, W. (1990). *Multi-problem screening inventory*. Tempe, AZ: Walmyr.

Hudson, W. (1992). *Walmyr assessment scales scoring manual.* Tempe, AZ; Walmyr.

Juran, J. (1989). *Juran on leadership for quality. An executive handbook.* New York: The Free Press.

Kettner, P., & Martin, L. L. (1993). Performance, accountability and purchase of service contracting. *Administration in Social Work, 17,* 61–79.

Kettner, P., Moroney, R., & Martin, L. L. (2008). *Designing and managing programs: An effectiveness-based approach.* Thousand Oaks, CA: Sage.

Kuechler, C., Velasquez, J., & White, M. (1988). An assessment of human service program measures: Are they credible, feasible, useful? *Administration in Social Work, 12,* 71–89.

Labaw, P. (1980). *Advanced questionnaire design.* Cambridge, MA: Abt.

Martin, L. L. (1993a). *Total quality management in human service organizations.* Newbury Park, CA: Sage.

Martin, L. L. (1993b). Total quality management: The new managerial wave. *Administration in Social Work, 17,* 1–16.

Martin, L. L. (2001). *Financial management for human service administrators.* Boston, MA: Allyn & Bacon.

Martin, L. L. (2002). *Performance-based contracting: What the federal government can learn from state and local governments.* Washington, DC: The IBM Center for the Business of Government. Retrieved April 15, 2008, from www.businessof government.org

Martin, L. L. (2005). Performance-based contracting for human services: Does it work? *Administration in Social Work, 29,* 63–77.

Martin, L. L. (2007). Performance-based contracting for human services: A proposed model. *Public Administration Quarterly, 31,* 130–158.

Martin, L. L. (2008). Program planning and management. In R. Patti (Ed.), *Handbook of human services* (pp. 339–350). Thousand Oaks, CA: Sage.

McDavid, J., & Hawthorn, L. (2006). *Program evaluation and performance measurement: An introduction to practice.* Thousand Oaks, CA: Sage.

Melkers, J., & Willoughby, K. (1998). The state of the states: Performance budgeting in 47 out of 50. *Public Administration Review, 58,* 66–71.

Millar, A., Hatry, H., & Koss, M. (1977a). *Monitoring the outcomes of social services. Vol. 1: Preliminary suggestions.* Washington, DC: Urban Institute.

Millar, A., Hatry, H., & Koss, M. (1977b). *Monitoring the outcomes of social services. Vol. 2: A review of past research and test activities.* Washington, DC: Urban Institute.

Millar, R., & Millar, A. (Eds.). (1981). *Developing client outcome monitoring systems: A guide for state and local social service agencies.* Washington, DC: Urban Institute.

Miller, D. C. (1991). *Handbook of research design and social measurement* (5th ed.). Newbury Park, CA: Sage.

Mulvaney, R., Zwahr, M., & Baranowski, L. (2006). The trend toward accountability: What does it mean for HR managers? *Human Resources Management Review, 16,* 431–442.

Myers, S., Smith, H., & Martin, L. L. (2006). Conducting best practices research in public affairs. *International Journal of Public Policy, 1*(4), 367–378.

Netting, F., Kettner, P., & McMurtry, S. (2008). *Social work macro practice* (4th ed.). Boston: Pearson.

Nurius, P., & Hudson, W. (1993). *Human services: Practice, evaluation and computers.* Pacific Grove, CA: Brooks/Cole.

Poertner, J. (2008). Managing for service outcomes: The critical role of information. *The handbook of human services management.* Thousand Oaks, CA: Sage.

Posavac, C., & Carey, R. (1997). *Program evaluation: Methods and case students* (5th ed.). Upper Saddle River, NJ: Prentice-Hall.

Pruger, R., & Miller, L. (1991). Efficiency and the social services: Part A. *Administration in Social Work, 15,* 5–24.

Rocheleau, B. (1988). Linking services to program goals: Two different worlds of program evaluation. *Public Administration Review, 12,* 92–114.

Rosenberg, M., & Brody, R. (1974). *Systems service people.* Cleveland, OH: Case Western Reserve School of Applied Social Sciences.

Rossi, P., Lipsey, M., & Freeman, H. (2004). *Evaluation: A systematic approach* (7th ed.). Thousand Oaks, CA: Sage.

Schainblatt, A. (1977). *Monitoring the outcomes of state mental health treatment programs: Some initial suggestions.* Washington, DC: Urban Institute.

Smith, R., & Lynch, T. (2004). *Public budgeting in America* (5th ed.). Englewood Cliffs, NJ: Prentice-Hall.

Speer, D. (1977). An evaluation of the Denver Community Health Questionnaire as a measure of outpatient treatment effectiveness. *Evaluation Review, 1*(3), 475–492.

Steering Committee for the Review of Government Service Provision. (2007). *Report on government services 2007.* Canberra, Australia: Productivity Commission.

Tatara, T. (1980). *A report of the national conference on client outcome monitoring procedures for social services.* Washington, DC: American Public Welfare Association.

United Way of America. (1996a). *Focusing on program outcomes: Summary guide.* Alexandria, VA: Author.

United Way of America. (1996b). *Measuring program outcomes: A practical approach.* Alexandria, VA: Author.

United Way of America. (2003). *Outcome measurement in national health and human service and accrediting organizations.* Alexandria, VA: Author.

United Way of America. (2006). *Outcomes measurement resource network.* Alexandria, VA: Author.

University of Wisconsin–Extension. (2003). *Logic model.* Retrieved August 8, 2008, from www.uwex.edu/ces/pdande/

Urban Institute. (1980). *Performance measurement.* Washington, DC: Author.

Urban Institute. (2002). *Findings from a symposium: How and why nonprofits use outcome information.* Retrieved August 8, 2008, from www.urban/org/UploadedPDF/310464HowAndWhy.pdf

U.S. Department of Health and Human Services. (2008). *Appendix B: Child welfare outcomes and measures.* Washington, DC: U.S. Department of Health and Human Services, Children's Bureau, Administration for Children and Families. Retrieved July 7, 2008, from www.acf.hhs.gov/prorams/cb/pubs/cw003/appendixb.htm

U.S. Department of Labor. (2008). *Workforce Investment Act (WIA) performance measures.* Washington, DC: U.S. Department of Labor, Employment and Training Administration. Retrieved July 7, 2008, from www.doleta.gov/Performance/quickview/WIAPMeasures.cfm

Virginia Tech. (2008). *Statistics activity-based learning environment.* Retrieved August 26, 2008, from http://simon.cs.vt.edu/SoSci/converted?Measurement/activity.html

Workforce Investment Act of 1998, Pub. L. No. 105-220, 112 Stat. 936.

Wye, C. (2002). *Performance management: A "start where you are, use what you have" guide.* Washington, DC: IBM Center for the Business of Government. Retrieved October 30, 2008, from www.businessofgovernment.org

Zhang, J., Mikovsky, L., & Martin, L. L. (2006). *A comparison of local government performance measurement systems.* Orlando: University of Central Florida, Center for Community Partnerships.

Zimmerman, J., & Stevens, B. (2006). The use of performance measurement in South Carolina nonprofits. *Nonprofit Management & Leadership, 16,* 315–327.

Index

Ables, P., 4, 47
Abuse
    adoption and safe families act
        and, 18t
    alcohol/drug, 29–30, 32, 33t, 37, 90
    children and, 29, 30, 34, 36t, 37
Accessibility, 52, 53t, 123, 126t
Accountants, 16, 22
Adoption and Safe Families Act, 18t
Adult day care
    numeric counts and, 83t
    program of services and, 75
    selecting units of service and,
        45–46, 47t
Advocacy groups
    LOF scales and, 102
    service efforts/accomplishments
        ratios and, 22
    social indicator data and, 71
Age issues, 67, 101t
Alcohol/drug abuse
    causes of, 29–30
    child abuse and, 37
    logic models and, 32, 33t
    methamphetamines and, 31, 32, 33t
    standardized measures and, 90
American Public Welfare Association
    (APWA), 2
Anger, 108
Anthony, R., 30, 31
Anxiety, 97
Aptitude, 90, 91t

Area Agency on Aging (AAA), 34, 35t
Arizona Self-Sufficiency Matrix,
    8, 73, 74t
At-risk elderly
    adult day care and, 75 .*See also*
        Adult day care
    elderly neglect and, 29
    logic models and, 34, 35t,
        36t, 37, 122t
Attitudes
    numeric counts and, 80
    outcome performance measures
        and, 65–66, 123
    quality-of-life changes and, 64
    standardized measures and,
        67, 88, 90, 91t, 92, 95
Auditors, 16, 22

Babbie, E., 100
Baranowski, L., 2
Benveniste, G., 68
Bickman, L., 100
Bliss, D., 2, 11, 17, 25
Block grants, 29
    See also Funding
Bloom, M., 90
Boredom, 108
Bowers, G., 41, 42
Bowers, M., 41, 42
Brody, R., 4, 40, 42
Budgets, 3, 30, 31
    See also Costs

Note: In page references, f indicates figures and t indicates tables.

California Department of Community
    Services and Development, 104
Carey, R., 88, 93
Carmeli, A., 4
Carter, R., 64
Case management
    ICM and, 120, 124t, 126, 127t, 128
    numeric counts and, 83t
    outcome performance measures
        and, 123
    output performance measures and,
        49–50
    successful case closure and, 84
Cause-and-effect relationships, 32
    effectiveness perspectives and, 8
    human service programs/social
        indicators and, 73
    numeric counts and, 81, 85
    outcome performance measures
        and, 69–71, 73, 75, 76
    social indicators and, 73, 75
Child abuse
    causes of, 30
    funding and, 29
    logic models and, 34, 36t, 37
    program design and, 32
Child care
    funding and, 29
    intermediate output performance
        measures and, 42
    LOF scales and, 102, 103t
    standardized measures and, 90
Child Care, Inc., 34, 37
Child Protective Services (CPS), 120
    logic models and, 36t, 37
    program design and, 32
Child welfare, 83t, 124–125
Citizens
    LOF scales and, 102
    service efforts/accomplishments
        ratios and, 22
    social indicator data and, 71
Client outcomes. *See* Outcome
    performance measures
Client satisfaction, 113–118
    LOF scales and, 112
    numeric counts and, 84, 86

outcome performance measures
    and, 66–67, 66t, 68t, 76, 78
overview of performance measures
    and, 24t
performance measures and, 55, 56t,
    58–61, 66, 67, 68
quality-of-life changes and, 123
quality performance measures
    and, 17
survey/questionnaire and, 60t,
    113–114, 114t, 116–117
UE and, 126t
Clinical cutting score,
    90, 92, 95, 110
Community Development Block
    Grant (CDBG), 29
Community problems
    assumptions and, 29–30
    logic models and, 26–28, 26f,
        28, 34, 35t
    program design and, 32
Community support, 28
Confidentiality, 86
Congress, 14
Consensus
    assessing outcome performance
        measures and, 69
    selecting units of service and,
        43, 45, 46t
Contact units of service
    intermediate output performance
        measures and, 42, 43, 45
    overview of performance measures
        and, 24t
    See also Units of service
Corcoran, K., 93
Cosenza, C., 105, 109
Costs
    client satisfaction and, 115, 116, 116t,
        117, 117t
    LOF scales and, 111, 111t, 112
    numeric counts and, 84, 85t, 86
    outcome performance measures
        and, 76, 77t, 78
    standardized measures and,
        97, 97t
Council on Accreditation, 17

Counseling
    client satisfaction and, 58–59, 58t,
        114, 114t, 115
    client satisfaction survey
        questionnaire and, 60t
    CPS and, 120
    intermediate output performance
        measures and, 42
    LOF scales and, 108
    logic models and, 34, 37
    numeric counts and, 80, 80t,
        81, 82t, 86
    quality dimensions and,
        56, 57–58, 58, 59
    standardized measures and, 90
Crime, 29–30
Cronbach, L., 8
Crosby, P., 7, 51
Cycle time issues, 55, 57, 59

Dashboards, ix, 123–125
Data, 130
    client satisfaction and, 68, 113–114,
        114t, 115, 116, 117
    decision making and, 119, 125
    human service programs and, 4
    intermediate output performance
        measures and, 42
    LOF scales and, 107, 108, 109, 110, 112
    numeric counts and, 84, 85, 86, 95, 96
    outcome performance measures
        and, 17, 68, 76, 77, 78, 94
    program design and, 31
    quality performance measures
        and, 55
    quality programs and, 10
    resource allocation decisions and,
        10–11
    service completion and, 50
    social indicators and, 71
    standardized measures and, 88–89,
        89t, 96
    types of, 89t
    units of service and, 45, 46
Day care. See Adult day care; Child
    care
Deming, W., 7, 51

Department of Social Services,
    32, 34, 37
Descriptors
    LOF scales and, 100, 101, 102–105,
        109–110, 112
    standardized measures and, 92
Dimensions of functioning, 101
Disabled persons, 81
Dropouts/graduations,
    47, 50, 79
Drug abuse. See Alcohol/drug abuse

Effectiveness, 6t, 8–9, 128t
    absence of formally adopted
        measures of, 10
    GPRA and, 14–15
    performance-based contracting
        and, 19
    quality performance measures
        and, 17
    SEA reporting and, 20t
    service efforts/accomplishments
        ratios and, 23t
    systems model and, 5
Efficiency, 6–7, 6t, 128t, 130t
    absence of formally adopted
        measures of, 10
    effectiveness perspectives and, 9
    quality performance measures
        and, 17
    SEA reporting and, 16, 20t
    service efforts/accomplishments
        ratios and, 23t
    systems model and, 5
Efficiency trap, 51
Elderly neglect, 29
    See also Neglect
Elder Outreach program, 34, 35t
Elected officials, 22, 31, 71
Else, J., 64
Empathy, 5, 52, 53t, 54, 55, 56, 123
Employment, 121
    cause-and-effect relationships
        and, 70
    numeric counts and, 83
    UE and, 120, 126t, 127t
    unemployment and, 29–30, 73

Episode units of service, 23
   intermediate output performance
      measures and, 42, 42t, 57
   output performance measures
      and, 122
   overview of performance measures
      and, 24t
   parent training and, 125t
   SEA reports and, 129t
   service completions and, 48t, 49, 50
   See also Units of service
Epstein, I., 107, 110, 111
Ethical issues, 78, 86
Ethnicity, 67
Evaluations, program, 8
Expanded systems model, 4–5, 5f, 25,
   26f, 39, 40f

Feasibility issues
   client satisfaction and, 115–116, 116t,
      117, 117t
   LOF scales and, 111–112, 111t
   numeric counts and, 84, 85t, 86
   outcome performance measures
      and, 69, 76, 77t, 78, 117
   selecting units of service and,
      43, 45, 46t
   standardized measures and,
      96–97, 97t
Federal Acquisition Regulation (FAR),
   18, 19f
Federal funding *See* Funding
Feedback
   effectiveness perspectives and, 9
   efficiency perspectives and, 6
   LOF scales and, 108
   logic models and, 27–28
   output performance measures
      and, 39
   quality perspectives and, 8
   systems model and, 4, 5, 5f
Fee-for-service contracts, 7
Final outputs performance measures,
   40, 41f, 47–50, 67–68, 68t
   numeric counts and, 80, 81
   overview of, 23–24, 24t
   review of, 122

SEA reports and, 129t
See also Final outputs performance
   measures
Fischer, E., 4, 11, 17, 25, 43, 45
Fischer, J., 90, 93
Five-point scale, 102–103
For-profit organizations
   GPRA and, 15
   outcome performance measures
      and, 18
   SEA reporting and, 16
Foster care
   adoption and safe families act
      and, 18t
   numeric counts and, 80
   standardized measures and, 90
   units of service and, 44t
Foundations
   client satisfaction and, 115
   funding and, 1–2, 18, 31
   performance measurement and, 11
   performance measurement data
      and, 17
   program design and, 31
Fowler, F., 102, 105, 109
Franklin, C., 92
Freeman, H., 2, 50, 76, 100
Full-Time Equivalent (FTE), 128t, 130t
   SEA reporting and, 19, 20t, 21, 22
Funding, 1–2
   adopting performance
      accountability/measurement
      and, 9
   block grants and, 29
   drug abuse and, 32
   efficiency perspectives and, 7
   elderly and, 34
   goals/objectives and, 34, 37
   LOF scales and, 102
   logic models and, 34, 37
   numeric counts and, 84
   outcome performance measures
      and, 17, 18
   performance
      accountability/measurement
      and, 13, 18, 19
   program design and, 31, 32

quality performance measures and, 52
quality perspectives and, 7, 8
service efforts/accomplishments ratios and, 22
social problems and, 28–29, 34, 37

Gallagher, R., 2, 7
General Educational Development (GED), 121
Gilmour, J., 3, 14
Goals, 3
  efficiency perspectives and, 7
  logic models and, 34, 37
  program design and, 30
Governmental Accounting Standards Board (GASB), 8, 13, 15t, 126
  cause-and-effect relationships and, 69
  outcome performance measures and, 63–64, 78
  SEA reporting and, 16
Government Performance and Results Act (GPRA), 14–15, 15t, 39
  cause-and-effect relationships and, 71
  outcome performance measures and, 17
Graduations/dropouts, 47, 50, 79
Grants, 28, 32
  See also Funding
Groze, V., 64
Gunther, J., 7

Hatry, H., 64, 71
Hawkins, F., 7
Hawthorn, L., 2
Head Start/Voluntary Pre-K services, 28, 83t, 84
Health issues
  LOF scales and, 100, 101t
  program of services and, 75
  screening and, 47t
  standardized measures and, 90
Home delivered meals, 3, 8
  client satisfaction and, 114, 114t
  client satisfaction survey questionnaire and, 60t

numeric counts and, 80, 80t, 81, 82t, 115
quality dimensions and, 56, 57, 58t, 59
See also Meals for seniors
Homelessness, 27, 29, 77t, 83t
Hornby, H., 64
Housing, 11, 29, 64, 74t, 105, 106t
Hudson, W., 68, 76, 90, 91, 92, 96, 97, 106
Humaneness, 5, 52, 53t, 123
Human service agencies, 3, 7, 14, 129
  dashboards and, 123–124
  data and, 11
  efficiency and, 61
  funding and, 19
  (LOF) scales and, 99
  SEA reporting and, 21

Independence for Seniors, Inc., 34
Independent living, 35t, 81
Index of Marital Satisfaction, 92, 96
Information/referral service
  client satisfaction and, 114, 114t, 115
  numeric counts and, 80, 80t, 81, 82t
  quality dimensions and, 56
  units of service and, 42, 44t
Inputs
  effectiveness perspectives and, 9
  efficiency perspectives and, 6
  quality perspectives and, 8
  SEA reporting and, 19–21, 20t
  systems model and, 4, 5, 5f
Intensive Case Management (ICM), 120, 124t, 126, 127t, 128
  See also Case management
Intermediate outcome performance measures, 67–68, 68t
  numeric counts and, 80, 81
Intermediate output performance measures, 41–47, 41f
  review of, 122
  See also Units of service

Job placements, 70
Job training
  cause-and-effect relationships and, 70
  intermediate output performance measures and, 42

numeric counts and, 83, 83t
social problems and, 28
standardized measures and, 90
Juran, J., 7, 51

Kettner, P.
analyzing problems and, 101
budgeting and, 126
expanded systems model and, 4
logic models and, 28
numeric counts and, 79
outcome performance measures
and, 8, 64, 66, 68, 76, 78
process issues and, 2
quality performance measures
and, 17
service completion and, 47
Koss, M., 64
Kuechler, C., 66, 68, 76, 111

Labaw, P., 102
Level Of Functioning (LOF) scales,
99–112
numeric counts and, 84, 86
outcome performance measures
and, 66–67, 66t, 68t, 76, 78
quality-of-life changes and, 123
Level of measurement, 76–77
Likert-type scales, 91
Lipsey, M., 2, 50, 76, 100
Logic models, 24, 25–37, 130t
social problems and, 122t
Lynch, T., 3, 18, 31

Managed care programs, 7
Management services, 50, 84
Marital Communications Skills Rating
Scale, 92
Martin, L. L.
analyzing problems and, 101
budgeting and, 126
dashboards and, 123
data and, 119
funding and, 2
intermediate output performance
measures and, 42
logic models and, 26

low-quality services and, 7
numeric counts and, 79, 84
outcome performance measures
and, 64, 66, 68, 76, 78
performance accountability
and, 4
performance and, 18
performance-based contracting
and, 19
program definition and, 3
program design and, 30
quality and, 17, 52
SEA reporting and, 21
service completion and, 47
unit cost reporting and, 45
Material units of service
intermediate output performance
measures and, 42, 42t,
43, 45, 122
overview of performance measures
and, 24t
See also Units of service
McDavid, J., 2
McMurtry, S., 28
Meals for seniors
LOF scales and, 100, 101t
numeric counts and, 81
program of services and, 75
selecting units of service and,
45, 47t
social problems and, 28, 34
See also Home delivered meals
Melkers, J., 16, 18
Methamphetamines, 31, 32, 33t
See also Alcohol/drug abuse
Mikovsky, L., 84, 123
Millar, A., 2, 64, 76, 78, 79, 85
Millar, R., 2, 64, 76, 78, 79, 85
Miller, D. C., 71
Miller, L., 7
Mirr, R., 64
Moroney, R., 2, 17, 64, 79, 101, 126
Multi-Problem Screening Inventory
(MPSI), 90
Mulvaney, R., 2
Murphy, M., 4, 47
Myers, S., 119

National Academy of Public
   Administration, 71
Neglect
   adoption and safe families act
      and, 18t
   efficiency perspectives and, 7
   elderly, 29
   LOF scales and, 109
Netting, F., 28
Nonprofit organizations
   GPRA and, 15
   outcome performance measures
      and, 17, 18
   program design and, 31
Numeric counts, 79–86
   assessment of, 84–86, 85t
   client satisfaction and,
      115, 117–118, 117t
   examples of, 80t
   LOF scales and, 110
   outcome performance measures
      and, 66–67, 66t, 68t, 76, 78
   quality-of-life changes and, 123
   standardized measures and, 95–96
Nurius, P., 68, 76, 106

Observations
   LOF scales and, 103, 105, 107–108
   of parents, 34
   standardized measures and, 92–93
Office of Management and Budget
   (OMB), 14
Orme, J., 90
Outcome performance measures,
      17–19, 18t, 63–78
   client satisfaction and, 113–114
   effectiveness perspectives and, 9
   GPRA and, 14–15
   logic models and, 26, 27–28, 27f, 32,
      33t, 34, 35t, 36t, 37
   numeric counts and, 81–83, 82t, 84.
      See also Numeric counts
   performance-based contracting
      and, 19
   performance measures and,
      23–24, 24t
   planning and, 121–123

program design and, 31
review of, 123
SEA reporting and, 20t, 21, 22, 22t
service completion and, 50
service efforts/accomplishments
   ratios and, 22, 23t
systems model and, 4, 5, 5f
Output performance measures,
      39–40, 41f
   efficiency perspectives and, 6
   final, 40, 41f, 47–50. See also Final
      outputs performance measures
   intermediate, 40, 41–47, 41f, 122
   logic models and, 26, 27–28, 27f, 32,
      33t, 34, 35t, 36t, 37
   numeric counts and, 81–82, 82t
   performance measures and, 23–24
   planning and, 121–123
   program design and, 31
   quality perspectives and, 8
   review of, 122
   SEA reporting and, 19, 20t, 21, 22, 22t
   service efforts/accomplishments
      ratios and, 22, 23t
   systems model and, 4, 5, 5f
Outputs with quality dimensions, 24t,
      55–58, 56t, 59
   numeric counts and, 79, 81

Parental Skills Training (PST), 120
Parenting skills, 30, 36t, 37
Parent Training (PT), 125t, 127t
   intermediate output performance
      measures and, 42
   logic models and, 34, 36t, 37
Participation
   client satisfaction and, 113
   LOF scales and, 102, 103t
   numeric counts and, 85
Performance-based contracts, 7, 19
Performance cost ratios, 21
Personality traits, 88, 90, 91t
Planning, 121–123
   program design and, 30–32
Poertner, J., 40, 64
Political factors, 78, 86
   elected officials and, 22, 31, 71

Posavac, C., 88, 93
Poverty, 29–30
Precision
    assessing performance measures
        and, 76–77, 77t
    client satisfaction and, 115–116, 116t,
        117, 117t
    LOF scales and, 111–112, 111t
    numeric counts and, 84–86, 85t
    outcome performance measures
        and, 76–77, 77t, 117t
    standardized measures and,
        96–97, 97t
    units of service and, 43, 44–45,
        46t, 69
Program evaluations, 8
Programs of services, 45–46, 75
Pruger, R., 7

Quality management theory, 7–8
Quality-of-life changes
    client satisfaction and, 67, 113–114,
        115, 116, 117
    clinical cutting score and, 92
    numeric counts and, 79, 80, 83,
        85, 87
    outcome performance measures
        and, 64–67, 65t, 69, 76–77
    program of services and, 75
    review of, 123
    standardized measures and, 87–88,
        92, 95
Quality performance measures,
        6t, 7–8, 56–58, 56t
    absence of formally adopted
        measures of, 10
    effectiveness perspectives and, 9
    GPRA and, 14–15
    logic models and, 26, 27–28, 27f, 32,
        33t, 34, 35t, 36t
    numeric counts and, 81–82, 82t
    overview of performance measures
        and, 24t
    performance-based contracting
        and, 19
    performance measures and, 23–24
    planning and, 121–123

review of, 123
    SEA reporting and, 16, 20t
    service accomplishments and, 22t
    systems model and, 4, 5, 5f
    TQM and, 16–17
Questionnaires/surveys.
        See Surveys/questionnaires

Ratio scale, 89–90
Recidivism, 80
Recreation. See Socialization/
        recreation
Referrals. See Information/referral
        service
Regulations, 13, 18, 28, 29
Reliability, 92–93
    client satisfaction and, 115–116, 116t,
        117, 117t
    ICM and, 124t
    LOF scales and, 102, 104, 107, 108,
        109, 110, 111, 111t
    logic models and, 36t, 37
    numeric counts and, 84–85, 85t
    outcome performance measures
        and, 76, 77t, 78
    PT and, 125t
    quality performance measures
        and, 54–55, 54t, 56, 57, 58t,
        59, 123
    SEA reports and, 129t
    standardized measures and,
        90, 96, 97t
    validity and, 92–93
Residential treatment centers,
        49, 107–108
Resource allocation decisions, 10–11
Responsiveness
    logic models and, 35t
    quality performance measures
        and, 5, 54–55, 54t, 56, 57, 58t,
        59, 123
Riverview Family Services (RFS),
        120–121, 123, 125
Rocheleau, B., 8
Rog, D., 100
Rosenberg, M., 4
Rossi, P., 2, 4, 8, 50, 76, 100

Scales, 89–90, 91–92
  five-point, 102–103
  See also Level of functioning (LOF)
    scales
Schainblatt, A., 64
Self-sufficiency, 73, 75, 76
Senior Services, Inc., 34
Service accomplishments, 19, 20t,
  21–23, 21t, 22t, 23t
Service completion, 24, 47–50, 48t
  logic models and, 33t, 35t, 36t
  outcome performance measures
    and, 67
  output performance measures
    and, 122
  service efforts/accomplishments
    and, 22t, 23t
  See also Final outputs performance
    measures
Service Efforts and Accomplishments
    (SEA), 13, 19–23, 128t, 129t, 130t
  accomplishments ratios and,
    22, 23t
  GASB and, 15t, 16
  input elements and, 21t
  outcome performance measures
    and, 63–64
  overview of performance measures
    and, 24t
  performance elements and, 22t
  performance measures and, 23–24
  program design and, 31
  reporting, 78, 126
  service efforts and, 19–21
Service focus, 82–83
Smith, H., 119
Smith, R., 3, 18, 31
Social indicators, 71–75, 72t, 73–73t
Socialization/recreation
  adult day care and, 47t, 75, 83t. *See
    also* Adult day care
  intermediate output performance
    measures and, 42
  LOF scales and, 102, 103t, 108, 109
  numeric counts and, 83t
  program of services and, 75
  units of service and, 109

Social problems
  causes of, 29–30
  funding and, 28–29. *See also* Funding
  human service programs and, 29
  logic models and, 26–28, 26f, 27f, 28,
    34, 36t, 37
  program design and, 32
Social Services Block Grant (SSBG), 29
Speer, D., 93
Standardized measures, 87–97
  data and, 88–89, 89t .*See also* Data
  numeric counts and, 84, 86
  outcome performance measures
    and, 66–67, 66t, 68t, 76, 78
  quality-of-life changes and, 123
Steering Committee for the Review of
    Government Services Provision
    (SCRGSP), 71–73, 72–73t
Stevens, B., 2, 4
Stress, 32, 37, 89–90
Surveys/questionnaires, 55, 59–61,
    60t, 114t
  client satisfaction and, 113–114, 114t,
    116–117
  standardized measures and, 88–89
  training and, 93

Target level of improvement,
    95–96, 110
Tatara, T., 64, 76
Testing, 87–88, 110
Time units
  intermediate output performance
    measures and, 23, 42, 43,
    44, 45–46, 57, 124t, 126t
  overview of performance measures
    and, 24t
Total Quality Management (TQM),
    15t, 16–17
Training, 121, 128t
  cause-and-effect relationships
    and, 70
  LOF scales and, 108
  numeric counts and, 83t
  social indicators and, 73
  standardized measures and, 90
  standardized tests and, 93

Transportation, 3, 8, 17
  adult day care and, 47t
  logic models and, 35
  numeric counts and, 81
  ordinal data and, 88, 89t
  program of services and, 75
  quality performance measures
      and, 53t
  units of service and, 44t, 45
Tripodi, T., 107, 110, 111

Unemployment
  causes of, 29–30
  employment and, 70, 83, 121
  social indicators and, 73
Unit cost reporting
  client satisfaction and,
      115, 116t, 117, 117t
  LOF scales and, 111–112, 111t
  numeric counts and, 84, 85t, 86
  outcome performance measures
      and, 69, 76, 77t, 78, 117
  selecting units of service and,
      43, 45, 46t
  standardized measures and,
      96–97, 97t
United Way of America, 1–2, 14,
      17, 39, 67
Units of service, 41–42
  contact, 24t, 42, 43, 45
  material, 24t, 42, 42t, 43, 45, 122
  quality dimensions and, 56
  selecting, 43–45, 44t
  service efforts/accomplishments
      ratios and, 22
  types of, 42–43, 42t
  See also Episode units of service
University of Wisconsin–Extension,
      26, 68
Upgrading Employment (UE), 120,
      126t, 127t
Urban Institute, 4, 25
U.S. Census, 71

U.S. Department of Health and
      Human Services, 18, 34
U.S. Department of Labor, 18
Utility
  client satisfaction and, 115, 116t,
      117–118, 117t
  LOF scales and, 111–112, 111t
  numeric counts and, 84–86, 85t
  outcome performance measures
      and, 76, 77t, 117–118, 117t
  performance measures and, 76, 77t
  selecting a unit of service and,
      43–44, 45, 46t
  standardized measures and, 96, 97t

Validity, 92–93
  client satisfaction and, 115, 116t,
      117, 117t
  LOF scales and, 111, 111t
  numeric counts and, 84, 85, 85t, 86
  outcome performance measures
      and, 76, 77t, 78
  standardized measures and,
      90, 96, 97t
Velasquez, J., 66
Violence, 36t, 37, 90
Virginia Tech, 88

Waiting time issues, 55, 57, 59
Web sites, 93
  dashboards and, 124, 125
Wheetlock, 64
White, M., 66
Wholey, J., 71
Willoughby, K., 16, 18
Workforce Investment Act, 18
Wye, C., 119

Young, D., 30, 31

Zhang, J., 84, 123
Zimmerman, J., 2, 4
Zwahr, M., 2

About the Authors

Lawrence L. Martin is professor of public affairs, social work, and public administration at the University of Central Florida in Orlando. He was previously on the faculty of the Columbia University School of Social Work in New York City where he directed the program in social work administration. He is the author of 20 books and major monographs and over 100 articles and book chapters. His works have been translated and reprinted in Chinese, French, Korean, Portuguese, Russian, and Mongolian. He has also worked with governmental and nongovernmental organizations (NGOs) in several foreign countries.

Peter M. Kettner is professor emeritus at the Arizona State University School of Social Work. He is the author of six books, four of which have been translated into multiple languages. He has also authored over 50 articles, monographs, and book chapters on the topics of purchase-of-service contracting, privatization, macro practice in social work, human services planning, and social work administration. Over his 30-year career in academia, he served as a consultant to five different state human service agencies and dozens of local nonprofit agencies on their purchase-of-service contacting practices and in the design and implementation of effectiveness-based planning systems. In retirement he has continued his writing and consultation with local government and nonprofit agencies.